BUREAUCRACY it is OMNIPOTENT!

(second edition)

Ilya Kogan

ISBN-13: 978-1514713426
ISBN-10: 151471342X

This book shows (on the example of the USPTO of the USA) how a very important organization works for distracting the state (in this case USPTO works against the USA), instead of serving the USA. The book presents the views and interpretations of some facts about bureaucracy influence. First, relation or bureaucracy and corruption.

I filled an application. The application was registered in USPTO on January 13, 2005, number 10/905635. It has been more than 10 years, but it is not clear what deserve my application. The book is written not in support of the application, which the USPTO buried. **Nevertheless, I hope to receive from USPTO competent reviews rather than bureaucratic response, which is not related to the stated topic.**

Using an example of the USPTO work is shown how it harms the United States of America.

I believe that this is not a unique example. The actions of the USPTO and, unfortunately, others, who should safeguard the interests of the country, are similar to a single cohesive bureaucracy.

TABLE OF CONTENTS

PART ONE

1. PREFACE

This book is a supplement to the first edition. I suddenly received a letter from the USPTO, which is a consequence of accessing by them a note from the Office of the Attorney General. Surprise, a double surprise and news. I did not expect that the Prosecutor's Office would pay attention to my complaints because I received nothing from the Prosecutor's Office. I did not expect that the USPTO would send me a letter. A copy of the letter is below. I was not expected that in the letter the USPTO would reaffirm its commitment to the bureaucracy and confidence in its omnipotence.

More than 10 years ago, I filed and registered in the USPTO an application for invention (number 10/905635, January 13, 2005). In the "Soviet" period of my life, I have done such repeatedly and successfully. Since then, many years have passed. Computers and the Internet have emerged, which facilitate and speed up the paperwork.

Since I am a random client, my experience suggests that:

1. In the USPTO do not analyze, and probably do not read many coming applications. If there are cases where certain applications had a competent review, it does not disprove the facts below.

2. First and foremost, the USPTO seeks to ensure the work of the legal scope, which do service to the applicants. Of course at the expense of the applicants. Proof of this is the insistence of the USPTO to contact lawyers. While all items were rejected (allegedly) because they rewritten from other applications. However,

2.1. Ignored the fact that if there is no subject, no legal edit may not change this. I wrote about this in my responses.

2.2. I pointed out that the reviewer apparently did not read my application; either does not understand the crux of the matter. My application and proposal referenced by reviewer are fundamentally on different topics. Apparently, the USPTO reviewer does not read my answers.

3. I repeat, the USPTO reviewer does not read my answers. As can happen in a year (a YEAR!), I get an answer from the USPTO, which contains a copy of the previous review (photocopy) and a single mention about my response.

It is possible to continue, but the book contains materials that allow the reader to verify the methods of work of the USPTO.

Maybe not I alone had to deal with the bureaucracy. I thought it was peculiar only to states like the USSR. I was surprised to find that the state bureaucracy in the United States is even more powerful.

This work is dedicated to perpetuating in a monument the all-powerful bureaucracy of the United States. Reader, imagine trihedral column of silvery gray heavy-duty steel. On each face in gold is written:

BUREAUCRACY it is OMNIPOTENT!

If we combine these three copies of this book, then we obtain a model of the monument, reduced hundreds of times. Of course, the column is not empty and is on a strong foundation. Such a construction, as well as the bureaucracy itself is not afraid of any attack. It will survive any disasters.

Each proposal requires justification as the proposed column requires a foundation. For this purposes I have chosen one example that has sufficient qualities. The story continues for more than ten years (from January 2005) and is practically in a frozen state. Involved in it by actions (or inactions) are very high authorities, such as:

Attorney General of the United States, U.S. Department of Justice.

Secretary of U.S. Department of Commerce.

Under Secretary of Commerce, for Intellectual Property and Director, of the USPTO.

Many others, including mass media.

The problem is stiffened, and to move it from place is equivalent to move the million-ton monument, proposed above.

Why write this book?

Firstly, it is time to immortalize the omnipotence of the bureaucracy. This is my contribution to this issue.

Secondly, I want to present a copy to personas, particularly contributing to its emergence. Some have contributed by their actions as e.g. the USPTO. Others contribute through their inaction, such as, U.S. Department of Justice, the U.S. Department of Commerce, or mass media. I cannot say what more contributes to the omnipotence of the bureaucracy actions of the firsts, or the inaction of the seconds.

Thirdly, I want to thank everyone who has inspired me for this job. This does not contradict the desire to stop this outrage. Everyone who becomes a senior citizen faces a problem: what to do with himself. Thanks to them, I do not have this problem.

Yet one more reason exists. For more than ten years, my application is apparently lost its relevance. **Nevertheless, I am interested to get a competent review of my work. I am looking forward for getting it.** However, at my age this is unusual, even strange.

The second part of the book is a copy of the first edition that allows seeing documents without accessing the Internet. The first part summarizes the events of the past five years. I am almost forget this story. However, a letter from the USPTO slightly revived it. I am grateful to the USPTO for such a gift.

To be continued ... maybe.

2. BUREAUCRACY IS THE PROGENITOR OF CORRUPTION

About bureaucracy and corruption is written a lot. These phenomena are reflected in literature, art and science. Regularly studies are conducted and are printed rank of countries by level of corruption. However, there is no parallel tables with proliferation and rank of bureaucracy.

What is corruption? It is compensation for a rapid and favorable solution.

What is bureaucracy? This is procrastination of issues. These are various excuses and obstacles posed by officials on the ways to resolve the matters. Initially it may be for a variety of reasons. Here is laziness and negligence in their duties. Under qualification plays a significant role, which prevents to understand the issue. The significant role played by the high arrogance of bureaucrat.

Gradually it intersects and blends in one almost irresistible site. The matter, sometimes very important and interesting for the client, was stalled.

However, often these cases have a financial side. In this case, the client is looking for ways to speed up more energetically the problem.

The decision is obvious it begs itself. There must be a favorable relation of bureaucrat. This is done in different ways, however old as the world. The compliments, invitation bureaucrat to luxury resorts, where conditions are created that will appeal to the bureaucrat. Finally are hush money.

Thus, corruption is the result of bureaucracy. Corruption necessarily is preceded and accompanied by bureaucracy. These phenomena will necessarily accompany the hostility to the State and society, which they are supposed to serve. For the sake of own interests bureaucrats and corruptions officials are ready to inflict any damage to the State, which they are supposed to serve as officials of that State.

Often the bureaucracy itself is organized in a circular complicity to support their actions. While not necessarily it is expressed in active actions to support bureaucrats. More often, this is something as self-destruction from combat the bureaucracy. Here it is especially important self-removal of organs, which are obliged to combat this phenomenon. It is, primarily, the public prosecutor's Office, State supervision, Congress, and the media.

For example, not necessarily to organize the fight against weeds or pests in a garden. Enough not to pay attention to it and they for sure will ruin a vegetable garden.

In my case, this is all there.

I have filed an application for an invention and paid all the appropriate fees (application number 10/905635, registered on January 13, 2005). Imaginably this is a dead-end, useless and not an original idea.

Almost three years have passed and I got the first answer. (USPTO **10/22/2007** Non-Final Rejection. (*This is the date of USPTO first reaction.*) ***It passed 2 year and 10 month.***)

In the reply (review), the USPTO rejected all items (exactly all!) of my proposal, as contained in other applications.

I mailed the response in some 2 weeks, on 11-12-2007. (**11-16-2007** Response to Non-Final Rejection).

The reason for such a quick response was no necessity to analyze the USPTO text. It has nothing to do with reality.

Analysis of the USPTO review allows you to conclude that it is a formal letter, which has nothing to do with the matter. It is clear that the reviewer did not understand the essence of my application. However, further indicates that the service acted as the omnipotent USPTO bureaucracy that is beyond criticism. However, I answered all the points in detail as if it was a serious letter. As if it was written by a person who seriously performs his duties, even it was obvious that it is not the case.

However, on **08-29-2008** USPTO sent me a Final Rejection. **In 9 month, USPTO on 10-22-2007 mailed a copy of the first answer.** *The only difference was that* ***it was a final rejection.*** *All the text was copied from the first answer.* My answer to the first review was ignored as if it was not existed.

I ask the reader to overthink this and evaluate actions of the USPTO. Nine months it took to make a copy (the exact photocopy) of its first response. However, one difference was, the answer was definite – it was a final rejection. No mention of my response to the first review was not in this initial response (the photocopy).

All documents are presented in the second part of the book and on the USPTO website.

As I found out dates of the answers correspond to the USPTO rules; there is a deadline, after which you can give a final refusal. Bureaucrats honor code.

I was able to achieve to reverse the final decision. Nevertheless, it did not change the essence of the action of the bureaucrats. After some "standard" period, I got a new final rejection.

Who could agree that to a clearly reasonable (not necessarily may be patented) application, there would such an answer - a formal unsubscribing, which does not relate to the substance of the issue. From that time, monthly I remind the USPTO and to a number of organizations whose inaction contributed to the development of bureaucracy that inevitably breeds corruption. I am posting these reminders by email. Section **6** provides an example of such a reminder.

On June 17 2015, to me (unexpectedly) was sent a letter from the USPTO (the copy of the letter in the section 3). From the letter, I realized that apparently the Prosecutor's Office sent a copy of my letter for help to the USPTO. From the letter follows that the USPTO is not going to fulfill their direct duties and finally write a sensible and reasonable review to my application. The USPTO requires additional payments, which will start the matter as if from beginning. That is, the prehistory is erased. However, the USPTO must first fix its wrong doings. I recall that this already paid by me.

I am prompted to pay for a new bureaucratic procedure. Like any bureaucracy, the USPTO is confident in its relevance and inerrancy of its arbitrariness.

My requirement are clear.

- USPTO is obliged to write a competent and reasonable review.

- USPTO in its reply is obliged to consider my objections and respond to them.

- USPTO does not have the right to demand payment from me for new procedures. I have already paid for the actions mentioned above.

- USPTO must cancel all its decisions taken earlier. All the old decisions nave no background.

3. USPTO LETTER FROM JUNE 17, 2015

United States Patent and Trademark Office

Office of the Commissioner for Patents

JUN 17 2015

Mr. Ilya Kogan
2573 E 27 St.
Brooklyn, NY 11235
kogani@optonline.net

Dear Mr. Kogan:

Re: Your Email About USPTO Work and Its Supporters

Thank you for your email to Attorney General of the United States, Eric H. Holder Jr. Your email has been forwarded to the U.S. Patent and Trademark Office (USPTO) and in particular, to the USPTO's Office of the Commissioner for Patents for a response.

In your email, you state:

> In January 2005, I submitted an application for an invention (application #10/905,635, filled 01/13/2005). During followed discussion, I obtained the incontestable evidence and demonstrated that USPTO carries out purposeful actions, which objectively cause:
>
> 1. The USPTO work does irreparable harm to the United States of America. Tremendous delays in analyzing the applications lead to,
> - Great financial damages caused by delay in the implementing of new technologies;
> - It is contributing to the technological backwardness of the United States.
> This is a huge moral damage to the country.

Kogan Email, March 29, 2015.

A review of the file history of application # 10/905,635 indicates that a Notice of Abandonment was mailed by the Office on December 9, 2010, for failure to properly respond to the final office action mailed on May 17, 2010.

§I. Revival of a Patent Application Based On Unintentional Delay

In order to continue the prosecution of this patent application, this application must first be revived. To revive an abandoned patent application, you must also submit a petition for revival

P.O. Box 1450, Alexandria, VA 22313-1450 • www.uspto.gov

2

based on unintentional delay with the appropriate petition fee. Additional information on a petition for revival based on unintentional delay can be found on our Web site: http://www.uspto.gov/patents-application-process/petitions/09-revival-based-unintentional-delay

As an initial matter, the general requirements of any petition can be found here: http://www.uspto.gov/about/offices/patents/pep/office_of_petitions.jsp#heading-1

1. Ways To File A Petition For Revival Based On Unintentional Delay

There are currently two ways to file a petition for revival based on unintentional delay. The two ways are: (1) e-petition; and (2) other methods including the postal mail.

(A) e-Petition for Revival Based on Unintentional Delay
EFS-Web Quick Start Guide for EFS-Web Petitions:
http://www.uspto.gov/sites/default/files/patents/process/file/efs/guidance/epetition-quickstart.pdf

(B) Other Methods Including the Postal Mail
To assist you with this method, you may use form (PTO/SB/64) titled "Petition For Revival Of An Application For Patent Abandoned Unintentionally Under 37 CFR 1.137(B)." A copy of form PTO/SB/64 is available at our website at:
http://www.uspto.gov/sites/default/files/web/forms/sb0064.pdf

2. Fees Associated With A Petition For Revival Based On Unintentional Delay

Along with your petition to revive based on unintentional delay, you must also pay the appropriate petition fee. Table 1 below lists the current fees for a petition to revive based on unintentional delay:

Column A	Column B	Column C	Column D	Column E
37 C.F.R. §	**Fee Description**	**Fee (or 'Large Entity' Fee)**	**'Small Entity' Fee**	**'Micro Entity' Fee**
1.17 (m)	Petition to Revive	$1,700	$850	$850

Table 1 – Fees for Petition to Revive Based on Unintentional Delay: All fees are subject to change.[1] Column titles (*e.g.* "Column A") are for reference purposes only.

For example, should you maintain small entity status, the petition fee for a 'Petition to Revive Based on Unintentional Delay' would be set forth in Column 'D' (*i.e.* $850). For additional guidance on a petition to revive for unintentional delay, see MPEP § 711.03(c), II., A., 2. (b). (Link to MPEP: http://www.uspto.gov/web/offices/pac/mpep/s711.html#d0e81972).

§II. Delays in Your Office Action

[1] While the fees in Table 1 are current as of June 2, 2015, please remember that all fees are subject to change. To get the latest list of fees and payments from Table 1 and for all other fee tables in this letter, go to the USPTO website titled "USPTO Fee Schedule" at: http://www.uspto.gov/learning-and-resources/fees-and-payment/uspto-fee schedule . Note that 'Column A' from Table 1 in this letter is the same as column titled "37 CFR" on the USPTO Fee Schedule website.

With regard to your concern about the delays in your Office actions, we consulted the Technology Center management where your application was examined. We found no evidence of abuse of the patent prosecution process. The prosecution history of this application shows that there is no indication that USPTO personnel have engaged in any deliberately inappropriate conduct in their handling of this application. Moreover, a review of our records indicates that the issues you raised within your letter have been addressed in previous communications from the Office.

§III. Additional Assistance

Finally, please be aware that the USPTO has many avenues for assistance for applicants. One of these avenues is our Inventors Assistance Center (IAC), information of which may be found on our Web site at: http://www.uspto.gov/inventors/iac/index.jsp.

The ICA is available between the hours of 8:30 a.m. – 5:00 p.m. (ET), Monday thru Friday at 800-PTO-9199 (800-786-9199) or 571-272-1000 (TTY customers can dial 571-272-9950 for customer assistance).

Additionally, the following links to our Web site (uspto.gov) contain valuable information that you can review before filing a patent application:
http://www.uspto.gov/faq/patents.jsp - Patent FAQs

I hope this letter addresses your concerns. If you have any further questions specific to this matter, please contact Andrew J. Fischer at (571) 272-8800.

Sincerely,

Anthony Caputa
Office of the Commissioner for Patent

4. THE CONCLUSION

Read and do not believe. The reader may also encounter the same feeling. However, all of the material available on the USPTO website, http://www.uspto.gov search for application # 10/905.635. That is all could be verified.

Why do I not believe? Of the materials follows,

- **USPTO simply idles**. How else can one explain that in the preparation a review, which is a copy of the previous one and which totally ignores and does not even mention the objections the applicant wrote, required approximately one year.

- **USPTO squanders money of claimants.** Because the review is paid by the applicant.

- **USPTO directs the work of illiterate or unfair reviewers.** How else can you explain that the reviews texts are inconsistent with the content of the applications reviewed? Even the theme of applications do not match.

- **USPTO are not even interested in common sense in its reviews.** For example, how can one explain the following? In review are rejected all (exactly all) points of the application because these items are already claimed by others. Nevertheless,

USPTO strongly recommend contacting lawyers. Is it possible that a legal revision could make the alleged patent items fit? This is similar to the demand for payment by the applicant of legal services, when USPTO knows (for sure knows) you do not need it.

There are mentioned only some of the phenomena, but they are all prerequisites for the development of corruption. Exactly such bureaucratic phenomena are progenitors of corruption.

Nevertheless, all this exists because of the implicit support of the whole bureaucracy, beyond the USPTO. Only this can explain the confidence of the USPTO in the impunity of such acts.

This primarily concerns the public prosecutor's Office and certain commissions of the Congress of the United States of America. However, the media play an "excessive" part.

If it were related only to several applicants, or me it would be a private matter. However, the delay for years the grant of patents causes,

- Reducing the competitive abilities of the country.

- Leaving United States, primarily in the area of high technology.

- This leads to a significant loss in trade. Increasing trade deficit and State debt.

Finally, it provokes a rise of corruption, which corrodes the country from within. It is for this reason that we must fight with such blatant manifestation of the bureaucracy in the work of the USPTO.

This book is a request for initiation of investigation:

- Concerning actions causing huge financial and prestigious damage to the USA.

- On identification of motives and the reasons brought to such situation.

- On identification the ones creating such situation.

- On the influence of all the above on the level of corruption.

I hope that this publication would draw attention to this issue.

At the same time, I hope finally get a competent review of my application. I expect that this review will take into account my objections.

5. CHRONOLOGY

In 2004, I prepared an application for an invention, and in January 2005, it had been filed and registered with the USPTO. In this section, in ascending order of dates are listed the major events related to the consideration of my application with the USPTO. The list (see part two) includes all USPTO materials, associated with the work related to the application. In the list are mentioned significant letters and materials that are not reflected on the USPTO website. At the beginning of the line in brackets is shown the section of part two where you can view the mentioned documents.

Materials themselves are placed in a separate chapter. In this chapter are many repetitions. This is due to the repetitions made by USPTO. If I write about it and do not give evidence, the reader would not believe that the USPTO copied material from one document into the next document. It would more correct to say that are copied the documents. The reader does not believe that such a copying for the USPTO officials takes about a year. However, this, all the materials and dates can be checked on the USPTO site.

In some cases, I have sent letters to other instances and copies of the letters were sent to the USPTO by e-mail. USPTO sent me an e-mail confirmation of the type, «Thank you for contacting the USPTO Contact Center. We have forwarded your inquiry to the appropriate special program office». Similar notices I received from the mass media. It was the same reaction with a rare exception. These materials are not included in the chronology.

Analysis of the dates shows that more than six years passed from January 2005. I want to emphasize that the time after the USPTO last answer is not considered. After six years, of which I have used three months for my answers, and the rest (about six years) was used by USPTO, I have not received any critical comments on the merits of my proposal. **Thus, after six years impossible to say what deserves my application.** As seen from the accompanying materials, this time (about six year) USPTO used to copy their previous answers into the next ones (about a year for making a copy). The first answer was naturally not copied (partially).

The list of basic materials related to the application number 10/905635, registered on January 13, 2005.

(3.1) 10-22-2007 USPTO Non-Final Rejection. (*This is the date of USPTO first reaction.* ***It passed 2 year and 10 month.***)

(3.2) 11-16-2007 Response to Non-Final Rejection. ***(I mailed the response in some 2 weeks, on 11-12-2007****. The reason for such a quick response was no necessity to analyze the USPTO text. It has nothing to do with reality.)*

(3.3) 08-29-2008 USPTO Final Rejection. ***(In 9 month, USPTO on 10-22-2007 mailed a copy of the first answer.*** *The only difference was that it was a final rejection. All the text was copied from the first answer.)*

(3.4) 09-12-2008 Response to USPTO 08/29/2008

(3.5) Letter to Department of Commerce, sent 09-10-2008

(3.6) USPTO Document from 11-24-2008

(3.7) Reply to the USPTO Document from 11-24-2008, sent 12-05-2008

USPTO Letter from 02-25-2009. Thank you for contacting DoC ...

(3.8) 03-02-2009 USPTO Non-Final Rejection *(This is unexpected non-final rejection after USPTO final rejection from 08-29-2008)*

(3.9) 04-02-2009 Response to USPTO non-final rejection from 03-02-2009

(3.10) 05-17-2010 USPTO Final Rejection *(The Second final rejection.)*

(3.11) My response to USPTO document from **5/17/2010** sent 6/2/2010

(3.12) USPTO letter from **11-29-2010.**

(3.13) My response to the USPTO letter from **11-29-2010**

(3.14) 12-02-2010 USPTO Document

(3.15) My response to the USPTO document from 12/02/2010

(3.16) USPTO letter from 12/09/2010

(3.17) My response to the USPTO letter from 12/09/2010

(3.18) USPTO letter from 12/20/2010

(3.19) My response to the USPTO letter from 12/20/2010

(3.20) USPTO letter from 01/06/2011

(3.21) My response to the USPTO letter from 01/06/2011

01-20-2011 USPTO Letter. Thank you for contacting DoC ...

(3.22) Letter to Attorney General and WSJ sent 02/26/2011

6. OLD VERSION OF REMINDER AND REQUEST FOR HELP

The version below was sent (distributed) in the past.

To: webmaster@usdoj.gov, usptoinfo@uspto.gov, AskDOJ@usdoj.gov, a.murray@wsj.com, TheSec@doc.gov
Cc: kenneth.frankel@finnegan.com

About USPTO work and its supporters.

FORTY-FOURTH TIME

Every month from May 27 2011, I sent an E-mail. In the E-mail I remind that it must be corrected unjust made by USPTO.

I stress, any money must pay the ones, who did this, not me.

December 3, 2013

To: Attorney General of the United States Eric H. Holder Jr.
U.S. Department of Justice
950 Pennsylvania Avenue, NW
Washington, DC 20530-0001

From: Ilya Kogan
2573 E 27 St., Brooklyn NY 11235,
ivkog1@gmail.com, 646-657-3208

Re: USPTO work for damaging the USA

Your honesty,

In January 2005, I submitted an application for an invention (application #10/905,635, filled 01/13/2005). During followed discussion, I obtained the incontestable evidence and demonstrated that USPTO carries out purposeful actions, which objectively cause:

1. The USPTO work does irreparable harm to the United States of America. Tremendous delays in analyzing the applications lead to,

- Great financial damages caused by delay in the implementing of new technologies;

- It is contributing to the technological backwardness of the United States.

This is a huge moral damage to the country.

2. Because the USPTO actions cause a great economic and moral damage to the U.S. I appeal to you, hoping to stop such actions. I see no other methods to stop such arbitrariness, only prosecutors and mass media. I have repeatedly offered to create a commission that would investigate USPTO work, to determine the motives, effects and damage from such actions.

As it is shown, (my case is obviously not the only one) USPTO, not without a base, is sure that it can do this with impunity. Discussion of my demand proceeded about 7 years. From which no less than 6 years were used for preparation of "reviews" by employees of USPTO. All their reviews (except the first) were copies (photocopies) of previous one. In the reviews there were no answers to my objections, my objections were ignored. On production of the next photocopy, USPTO spent about a year. However, there was slight difference. If in the review my points, all without an exception, were rejected, in the following copy was added that the answer is final.

I understand that in the written is difficult to believe, but it is easy to verify it:

- All documents are published on the USPTO site http://www.uspto.gov , search for application #10/905,635.

- I published a book, "BUREAUCRACY it is OMNIPOTENT!" ISBN-10 1461051398, which is available on AMAZON http://www.amazon.com In the book is described and analyzed the case and all documents are provided. Now I prepare continuations.

Below I give two short examples of the USPTO work. In my answers, I cannot ignore the USPTO reviewer text, as they ignored my arguments in their "reviews". In the USPTO review without mentioning my objections the reviewer make a copy of the previous review. Next time, I cannot answer to the same text with something different. To my previous answer, I could add only astonishment that my objections were ignored.

EXAMPLE 1.

In the USPTO reviews is written. "**For claim 3,** *With respect to claim 3:* ***Meade discloses*** *a method according to claim 1 that* *allows to receive TV programs and videophone conversations on big TV or PC screens directly through the cellular phone* ***(parag. 0027)****, the cellular phones have such possibilities; today's TV does not; temporarily can be used a coaxial cable output from the cellular phone, or any other available in TV; in the nearest future all digital TV would have a USB input, a USB output from a cellular phone already exists* ***(parag. 0027).****"* The above quotation is an exact copy from my application, in which reviewer added words shown in bold.

However, Meade's parag. 0027 in the Knoble application (Pub. No.: US 2002/0068529A1 as it was published on June 6 2002) mentioned a different goal:

*[**0027**] For example, upon entry within a room, the mobile computing device can automatically perform these steps: identify an appliance like a TV; activate the TV; turn the TV to a channel carrying a favorite program; and select a preferred volume level. In the event that the favorite program is not being broadcast, the mobile computing device can supply its own content. In particular, the mobile computing device can retrieve an episode of that program or substitute a program from memory of the mobile computing device, transfer that stored program to the TV, and then command the appliance to play the program.*

EXAMPLE 2.

In the USPTO reviews is written. "On page 2 in pos. 2 is written, **"With respect to claim 1: *Knoble teaches*** *a method which allows with minor changes in the modern cellular phone and without any additional services to eliminate and simplify the usage of many electronics and communication devices of everyday life.* ***(Col. 1, parag. 0010-0011)"*"** The above quotation is an exact copy from my application, in which reviewer added words shown in bold.

There is no such expression in Knoble application "additional services to eliminate and simplify the usage of many electronic and communication devices of everyday life" in Col. 1, parag. 0010 - 0011. The goal of the Knoble invention is:

"[0010] Accordingly, it is an object of the invention to provide a system and method to permit consumers and businesses to avoid redundant telephone service and the costs that are associated with such redundancy.

[0011] In order to achieve the above and other objects of the invention, a method of converting a telephone system that has been connected to the public switched network for cellular usage includes, according to a first aspect of the invention, disconnecting the telephone system from the public switched network; providing an adapter unit that is constructed and arranged to connect to at least one cellular telephone at a first point of connection and to the telephone system at a second point of connection, the adapter including a converter for converting at least one signal from the cellular telephone to at least one signal that is appropriate for use by the telephone system and for converting at least one signal from the telephone system to a signal that is appropriate for use by the cellular telephone; and connecting the adapter unit to the telephone system.."

As it is seen from the text and images, the only Knoble goal is, to eliminate telephone lines and associated expenses. I do not mention the phone bill expenses in my application, because there are doubts whether the enlargement of cell phone expenses may compensate this. In the Knoble case is the additional cost of the controlling computer, to say nothing about the necessity to learn its usage. To achieve the goal Knoble proposes **a special device (equivalent to a specialized computer, which has all the features of a computer: CPU, keyboard, monitor, and many additional special devices)**. This control device should be placed between the cell phone and traditional phone**. Even then, without changes in the cell phone, which Knoble does not mention, it would be impossible to connect to USB. In addition, there is difficult to imagine a problem, which could not be solved by a specially designed computer system. Knoble did something different with this powerful system. In addition, he tells nothing about the structure of such an expensive system.**

From the explanations given above it is obvious that the rejection of claims 1 - 10 based on the Pub. No.: US 2003/0071117A1 is incorrect.

In addition to **final refusal because all points of my application are copied from other applications,** USPTO required to address to the lawyer (the list was given) for application text editing. However, what for to edit the text copied from other applications. Can this make the application text patentable? The all positions of my application are already finally rejected. Is this a requirement of payment to (their?) lawyers?

I repeat the desperate request about initiation of investigation:

- Concerning actions causing huge financial and prestigious damage to the USA.

- On identification of motives and the reasons brought to such situation.

- On identification the ones creating such situation.

Copy of this letter is sent by E-mail to places created (by their work, or their silence) such ugly situation in the USA.

Sincerely Ilya Kogan

2573 E 27 St, Brooklyn NY 11235
ivkog1@gmail.com
646/657-3208

7. REMINDER AND REQUEST FOR HELP (NEW VERSION)

The new version is required in connection with some of the changes that have occurred in recent years. For example, a reference to the new, revised edition of the book. In the list, there would be some new recipients.

To: webmaster@usdoj.gov, …

About USPTO work and its supporters, 150720

FORTY-FIFTH TIME

Sent **150720**, 150620, 150329, 150206, 141214, 141105, 141002, 140827, 140729, 140630, 140527, 140430, 140326, 140228, 140131, 131220, 131119, 131015, 130902, 130815, 130628, 130531, 130502, 130403, 130307, 130131, 130101, 121130, 121030, 120905, 120801, 120701, 120607, 120429, 120330, 120228, 120130, 111230, 111203, 111104, 111003, 110830, 110728, 110630, 110527

Every month from May 27 2011, I sent an E-mail. In the E-mail I remind that it must be corrected unjust made by USPTO.

I stress, any money must pay the ones, who did this, not me.

December 3, 2013

To: Attorney General of the United States
LORETTA E. LYNCH
U.S. Department of Justice
950 Pennsylvania Avenue, NW
Washington, DC 20530-0001

From: Ilya Kogan
2573 E 27 St., Brooklyn NY 11235,
ivkog1@gmail.com, 646-657-3208

Re: USPTO work for damaging the USA

Your honesty,

In January 2005, I submitted an application for an invention (application #10/905,635, filled 01/13/2005). During followed discussion, I obtained the incontestable evidence and demonstrated that USPTO carries out purposeful actions, which objectively cause:

1. The USPTO work does irreparable harm to the United States of America. Tremendous delays in analyzing the applications lead to,

- Great financial damages caused by delay in the implementing of new technologies;

- It is contributing to the technological backwardness of the United States.

This is a huge moral damage to the country.

2. Because the USPTO actions cause a great economic and moral damage to the U.S. I appeal to you, hoping to stop such actions. I see no other methods to stop such arbitrariness, only prosecutors and mass media.

3. I offer to create a commission that would investigate USPTO work, to determine the motives, effects and damage from such actions. In particular, the commission should estimate how such work contribute to rising corruption in the US.

As it is shown, (my case is obviously not the only one) USPTO, not without a base, is sure that it can do this with impunity. Discussion of my demand proceeded about 7 years. From which no less than 6 years were used for preparation of "reviews" by employees of USPTO. All their reviews (except the first) were copies (photocopies) of previous one. In the reviews there were no answers to my objections, my objections were ignored. On production of the next photocopy, USPTO spent about a year. However, there was slight difference. If in the review my points, all without an exception, were rejected, in the following copy was added that the answer is final.

I understand that in the written is difficult to believe, but it is easy to verify it:

- All documents are published on the USPTO site http://www.uspto.gov , search for application #10/905,635.

- I published a book, "BUREAUCRACY it is OMNIPOTENT! (second edition)" ISBN-10 151471342X, which is available on AMAZON. In the book is described and analyzed the case and all documents are provided.

Below I give two short examples of the USPTO work. In my answers, I cannot ignore the USPTO reviewer text, as they ignored my arguments in their "reviews". In the USPTO review without mentioning my objections the reviewer make a copy of the previous review. Next time, I cannot answer to the same text with something different. To my previous answer, I could add only astonishment that my objections were ignored.

EXAMPLE 1.

In the USPTO reviews is written. "**For claim 3,** <u>*With respect to claim 3:*</u>***Meade discloses*** *a method according to claim 1 that allows to receive TV programs and videophone conversations on big TV or PC screens directly through the cellular phone* ***(parag. 0027)****, the cellular phones have such possibilities; today's TV does not; temporarily can be used a coaxial cable output from the cellular phone, or any other available in TV; in the nearest future all digital TV would have a USB input, a USB output from a cellular phone already exists* ***(parag. 0027)."*** The above quotation is an exact copy from my application, in which reviewer added words shown in bold.

However, Meade's parag. 0027 in the Knoble application (Pub. No.: US 2002/0068529A1 as it was published on June 6 2002) mentioned a different goal:

*[**0027**] For example, upon entry within a room, the mobile computing device can automatically perform these steps: identify an appliance like a TV; activate the TV; turn the TV to a channel carrying a favorite program; and select a preferred volume level. In the event that the favorite program is not being broadcast, the mobile computing device can supply its own content. In particular, the mobile computing device can retrieve an episode of that program or substitute a program from memory of the mobile computing device, transfer that stored program to the TV, and then command the appliance to play the program.*

EXAMPLE 2.

In the USPTO reviews is written. "On page 2 in pos. 2 is written, **"With respect to claim 1:** ***Knoble teaches*** *a method which allows with minor changes in the modern cellular phone and without any additional services to eliminate and simplify the usage of many electronics and communication devices of everyday life.* ***(Col. 1, parag. 0010-0011)""*** The above quotation is an exact copy from my application, in which reviewer added words shown in bold.

There is no such expression in Knoble application "additional services to eliminate and simplify the usage of many electronic and communication devices of everyday life" in Col. 1, parag. 0010 - 0011. The goal of the Knoble invention is:

"[0010] Accordingly, it is an object of the invention to provide a system and method to permit consumers and businesses to avoid redundant telephone service and the costs that are associated with such redundancy.

[0011] In order to achieve the above and other objects of the invention, a method of converting a telephone system that has been connected to the public switched network for cellular usage includes, according to a first aspect of the invention, disconnecting the telephone system from the public switched network; providing an adapter unit that is constructed and arranged to connect to at least one cellular telephone at a first point of connection and to the telephone system at a second point of connection, the adapter including a converter for converting at least one signal from the cellular telephone to at least one signal that is appropriate for use by the telephone system and for converting at least one signal from the telephone system to a signal that is appropriate for use by the cellular telephone; and connecting the adapter unit to the telephone system.."

As it is seen from the text and images, the only Knoble goal is, to eliminate telephone lines and associated expenses. This has nothing to do with my proposal, which has completely different goal. In the Knoble case is the additional cost of the controlling computer, to say nothing about the necessity to learn its usage. To achieve the goal Knoble proposes **a special device (equivalent to a specialized computer, which has all the features of a computer: CPU, keyboard, monitor, and many additional special devices)**. This control device should be placed between the cell phone and traditional phone. **Even then, without changes in the cell phone, which Knoble does not mention, it would be impossible to connect to USB. In addition, there is difficult to imagine a problem, which could not be solved by a specially designed computer system. Knoble did something different with this powerful system. In**

addition, he tells nothing about the structure of such an expensive system.

From the explanations given above it is obvious that the rejection of claims 1 - 10 based on the Pub. No.: US 2003/0071117A1 is incorrect.

In addition to **final refusal because all points (without exception) of my application are copied from other applications,** USPTO required to address to the lawyer (the list was given) for application text editing. However, what for to edit the text copied from other applications. Can this make the application text patentable? The all positions of my application are already finally rejected. Is this a requirement of payment to (their?) lawyers?

I repeat the desperate request about initiation of investigation:

- Concerning actions causing huge financial and prestigious damage to the USA.

- On identification of motives and the reasons brought to such situation.

- On identification the ones creating such situation.

- On identification the influence of USPTO work for rising corruption.

Copy of this letter is sent by E-mail to places created (by their work, or their silence) such ugly situation in the USA.

Sincerely Ilya Kogan

2573 E 27 St, Brooklyn NY 11235
ivkog1@gmail.com
646/657-3208

PART TWO

BUREAUCRACY it is OMNIPOTENT!

Ilya Kogan

ISBN-13: 978-1461051398

ISBN-10: 1461051398

TABLE OF CONTENTS

1. PREFACE

Maybe not I alone had to deal with the bureaucracy. I thought it was peculiar only to states like the USSR. I was surprised to find that the state bureaucracy in the United States is even more powerful.

This work is dedicated to perpetuating in a monument the all-powerful bureaucracy of the United States. Reader, imagine trihedral column of silvery gray heavy-duty steel. On each face in gold is written:

BUREAUCRACY
it is
OMNIPOTENT!

If we combine these three books, then we obtain a model of the monument, reduced hundreds of times. Of course, the column is not empty and is on a strong foundation. Such a construction, as well as the bureaucracy itself is not afraid of any attack. It will survive any disasters.

Each proposal requires justification as the proposed column requires a foundation. For this purposes I have chosen one example that has sufficient qualities. The story continues for more than five years (from January 2005) and is practically in a frozen state. Involved in it by actions (or inactions) are very high authorities, such as:

Attorney General of the United States, U.S. Department of Justice.

Secretary of U.S. Department of Commerce.

Under Secretary of Commerce, for Intellectual Property and Director, of the USPTO.

Many others, such as mass media.

The problem is stiffened, and to move it from place is equivalent to move the million-ton monument, proposed above.

Why Write This Book?

Firstly, it is time to immortalize the omnipotence of the bureaucracy. This is my contribution to this issue. Moreover, I am not afraid to write to this great issue.

Secondly, I want to present a copy to personas, particularly contributing to its emergence. Some have contributed by their actions as e.g. the USPTO. Others contribute through their inaction, such as, U.S. Department of Justice, the U.S. Department of Commerce, or mass media. I cannot say what more contributes to the omnipotence of the bureaucracy actions of the firsts, or the inaction of the seconds.

Thirdly, I want to thank everyone who has inspired me for this job. This does not contradict the desire to stop this outrage. Everyone who becomes a senior citizen faces a problem:

what to do with himself. Thanks to them, I do not have this problem.

Yet one additional reason exists. For more than five years, my application is apparently lost its relevance. **Nevertheless, I am interested to get a competent review of my work.**

2. BUREAUCRACY AND ITS INFLUENCE

2.1. Bureaucracy and Society

The activity of bureaucracy is not indifferent to the society. It affects all the branches of the society existence. For some more than a quarter of a century in the United States I collected many cases of similar type. Here I relate to one of them.

This work is related to a particular case, the work of the USPTO. Here is shown, that in more than six years impossible to say what deserves a particular application. There is reason to believe that my case is not unique. Apparently, there is a type of applications in respect of which the USPTO operates in the same way.

This shows that the USPTO work does irreparable harm to the United States of America. This is done in addition to the harm to the inventors. Such tremendous delays lead to great financial damages caused by a delay in the introduction of new technologies; it is contributing to the technological backwardness of the United States. This is a huge moral and financial damage to the country.

The USPTO actions cause great economic and moral damage to the U.S. Here I appeal to stop such actions. I see no other methods to stop such arbitrariness, but apply to prosecutors and the mass media. I have repeatedly offered to create a commission that would investigate USPTO work, to determine the motives, effect and damage from such actions.

Enormous financial and moral damage, which follows from the USPTO actions, must be ended. **With this purpose, it is necessary to create a commission on the level of Congress and Attorney General, which would find out:**

1. The state and organization of the work of the USPTO.

2. The damage, which is brought by USPTO actions, to the economy and to the image of the USA. Simultaneously it would be good to compare how much this damage exceeds the damage from, for example, terrorism, including expenditures for preventing terrorist acts.

3. Whether this objectively existing damage is the result of intentional actions.

4. How the categorical demand of enormous payment to the lawyers is compulsory. To what extent this requirement is unselfish.

Such a commission would be the very beginning of work for preventing the omnipotence of bureaucracy.

2.2. CONFIRMING EXAMPLES

2.2.1. GENERAL REMARKS

Suppose some official had written a reason, according to which he believes that the position reviewed should be rejected. He argues that the proposed provision is contained in another application or patent. In this particular case, he cites (copied) my suggestion and at the beginning he adds words *"Meade discloses"* and then exact copy of my text.

This text is not present in the Meade application. There is nothing of the kind neither in content nor in form nor in common sense. To this reviewer remark, I answered that it is absent in the Meade application.

In his next review, the official copies his remark, which is a copy of my proposal with the same additional words. He did not notice my objections and copies the previous text with the words *"Meade discloses"* at the beginning. This is an exact copy of the text of the preceding review. The only difference from the previous review is the replacement of words **not-final rejection** with words **final rejection.**

In addition, in the USPTO reviews are repeated such phrases as: *"Modifying Knoble (application) with McZeal invention will help in saving money and reduce redundancy. "*, or *"Modifying Meade with McZeal invention will help in saving money and eliminate the use of some electronics equipment on a separate basis."*

Such phrases are used as an additional reason for rejecting the proposals. I believe that the reviewer knows in which way should be modified and combined the features, which the reviewer has in mind. There are many patents, which are based on well-known and long existing things, which were a subject of patenting in the past. It is wrong to reject something because it could be performed by combining with modification of something that already exists.

This continues from one review into the next review from year to year. The official is assured that no one could protest. He was confident that all the superior bureaucracy would support him.

Below are two examples in confirmation of the above.

2.2.2. EXAMPLE 1

In the paragraph 3.8. 03-02-2009, USPTO Non-Final Rejection, reader might see:

«With respect to claim 3:

Meade discloses *a method according to claim 1 that allows to receive TV programs and videophone conversations on big TV or PC screens directly through the cellular phone* ***(parag. 0027),*** *the cellular phones have such possibilities; today's TV does not; temporarily can be used a coaxial cable output from the cellular phone, or any other available in TV; in the nearest future all digital TV would have a USB input, a USB output from a cellular phone already exists* ***(parag. 0027).»***

In the given citation reviewer copied the text from my application and added the words given in bold. In my response, I quoted the text of the reviewer and section 0027, referred to by the reviewer. See paragraph 3.9.

3. For claim 3, *With respect to claim 3:Meade discloses a method according to claim 1 that allows to receive TV programs and videophone conversations on big TV or PC screens directly through the cellular phone* ***(parag. 0027)****, the cellular phones have such possibilities; today's TV does not; temporarily can be used a coaxial cable output from the cellular phone, or any other available in TV; in the nearest future all digital TV would have a USB input, a USB output from a cellular phone already exists* ***(parag. 0027).***

As reader can see, the Meade's parag. 0027 mentioned a different goal:

[0027] For example, upon entry within a room, the mobile computing device can automatically perform these steps: identify an

appliance like a TV; activate the TV; turn the TV to a channel carrying a favorite program; and select a preferred volume level. In the event that the favorite program is not being broadcast, the mobile computing device can supply its own content. In particular, the mobile computing device can retrieve an episode of that program or substitute a program from memory of the mobile computing device, transfer that stored program to the TV, and then command the appliance to play the program.

This I have to do for each reviewer's comment. After all, the reviewer in the same way rejected all my items. The reader can find such quotes for a dozen pages in chapter 3. The following is my natural conclusion:

From the explanations given above it is obvious that the rejection of claims 1 - 10 based on the Pub. No.: US 2003/0071117A1 is incorrect.

It seems the question is closed. However, the next review (Section 3.10. 05-17-2010 USPTO Final Rejection), which came in a year, and which differs from the first one by words "**Non-Final Rejection**" replaced by "**Final Rejection**" I have:

«**With respect to claim 3:**

Meade discloses a method according to claim 1 that allows to receive TV programs and videophone conversations on big TV or PC screens directly through the cellular phone **(parag. 0027),** the cellular phones have such possibilities; today's TV does not;

temporarily can be used a coaxial cable output from the cellular phone, or any other available in TV; in the nearest future all digital TV would have a USB input, a USB output from a cellular phone already exists **(parag. 0027)».**

In the above citation reviewer as before copied text from my application and added the words in bold. **Actually, it is**

copied from the previous reviewer's response. Since I cannot ignore the comments of the reviewer, I must to repeat to all the reviver's remarks. My answer is as previous; I quoted the text of the reviewer and the section 0027, referred to by the reviewer. See paragraph 3.11.

3. For claim 3, "*With respect to claim 3:Meade discloses a method according to claim 1 that allows to receive TV programs and videophone conversations on big TV or PC screens directly through the cellular phone* ***(parag. 0027)****, the cellular phones have such possibilities; today's TV does not; temporarily can be used a coaxial cable output from the cellular phone, or any other available in TV; in the nearest future all digital TV would have a USB input, a USB output from a cellular phone already exists* **(parag. 0027)".**

Page 4

However, Meade's parag. 0027 mentioned a different goal: "*[0027] For example, upon entry within a room, the mobile computing device can automatically perform these steps: identify an appliance like a TV; activate the TV; turn the TV to a channel carrying a favorite program; and select a preferred volume level. In the event that the favorite program is not being broadcast, the mobile computing device can supply its own content. In particular, the mobile computing device can retrieve an episode of that program or substitute a program from memory of the mobile computing device, transfer that stored program to the TV, and then command the appliance to play the program*".

This I have to do (and repeat) for each of the reviewer's comments. After all, is unacceptable to leave the reviewers' comments with no response.

2.2.3. EXAMPLE 2

In the USPTO letter from 11-29-2010 (See 3.12) is written, *"In reviewing your application we see that a final rejection was mailed on May 17, 2010 and a reply from you was received on June 7, 2010. Since the Office did not act on your reply until after November 17, 2010, your* ***application is now*** **abandoned**. ***We*** **apologize** ***for this delay."***

What one should expect after such a phrase? For example, USPTO cancels application-abandoned state, and starts a new examination of the application. At the same time would be considered the moral and possibly financial compensation for the harm I caused. However, in a letter is proposed another option. *«Specifically, there are two options available under 37 CPR §1.117 that may enable an applicant to have an abandoned application revived. ... petition may be filed ... The petition fee as set forth in § 1.17(1) (currently $270.00 for small entity; $540.00) ... The second option for revival ... $810.00 for small entity: $1,620.00 ... Since a final rejection was mailed on May 17, 2010, the claims in your application have been rejected at least twice. You therefore have the option of appealing ...».*

Thus, USPTO:
- not only violates its rules and admit the violation;
- not only writes reviews that have nothing to do with reality;
- not only ignores the applicants' responses, in which is shown the real situation with reviews;
- USPTO requires the claimant to requested the USPTO for forgiveness for their guilt. USPTO states that claimant must pay a penalty. **The claimant, doing this, agrees that not USPTO, it was he - the applicant guilty for the situation created by USPTO.**

Then in the letter is written, *«If you truly believe your claims to be patentable, you should follow the correct procedure and file an appeal»*.

Again, all is put upside down. By entering, each one believes that the application deserves to become a patent. The USPTO should determine this. I draw your attention that the USPTO work is not free. However, USPTO perform the work in such a way, that the work with an application takes many years. As the result, the implementation of new technologies is deferred for many years. The technologies may become obsolete and the USA lags behind other countries. **The economic and moral damage is tremendous. This influences the authority of the USA, enlarges the negative trade balance, increases unemployment, and much more.**

Less than a week is sufficient for the composition of such reviews. However, for the review from May 17, 2010 one day is too much. Its main difference from the previous one is in one word; instead of non-final, the rejection is final. Could the reader believe the facts? It looks impossible, but it is true. All the UPSTO conclusions do not really reject anything in my application. **That is why I could not add anything that defends my application or proofs that it deserves a patent.** Refuting anything not connected to the matter under discussion adds nothing. **However, it is impossible to agree with the USPTO Office Action Summaries to app. No. 10/905635.**

2.3. CHRONOLOGY

In 2004, I prepared an application for an invention, and in January 2005, it had been filed and registered with the USPTO. In this section, in ascending order of dates are listed the major events related to the consideration of my application with the USPTO. The list includes all USPTO materials, associated with the work related to the application. In the list are mentioned significant letters and materials that are not reflected on the USPTO website. At the beginning of the line in brackets is shown the section where you can view the mentioned documents.

Materials themselves are placed in a separate chapter. In this chapter are many repetitions. This is due to the repetitions made by USPTO. If I write about it and do not give evidence, the reader would not believe that the USPTO copied material from one document into the next document. The reader does not believe that such a copying for the USPTO officials takes about a year. However, this, all the materials and dates can be checked on the USPTO site.

In some cases, I have sent letters to other instances and copies of the letters were sent to the USPTO by e-mail. USPTO sent me an e-mail confirmation of the type, «Thank you for contacting the USPTO Contact Center. We have forwarded your inquiry to the appropriate special program office». Similar notices I received from the mass media. It was the same reaction with a rare exception. These materials are not included in the chronology.

Analysis of the dates shows that more than six years passed from January 2005. I want to emphasize that the time after the USPTO last answer is not considered. After six years, of which I have used three months for my answers, and the rest (about six years) was used by USPTO, I have not received any critical comments on the merits of my proposal. **Thus, after six years impossible to say what deserves my application.** As seen from the accompanying materials, this time (about six year) USPTO used to copy their previous answers into the next ones (about a year for making a copy). The first answer was naturally not copied (partially).

The list of basic materials related to the application number 10/905635, registered on January 13, 2005.

(3.1) 10-22-2007 USPTO Non-Final Rejection. (*This is the date of USPTO first reaction.* ***It passed 2 year and 10 month.***)

(3.2) 11-16-2007 Response to Non-Final Rejection. ***(I mailed the response in some 2 weeks, on 11-12-2007****. The reason for such a quick response was no necessity to analyze the USPTO text. It has nothing to do with reality.)*

(3.3) 08-29-2008 USPTO Final Rejection. ***(In 9 month, USPTO on 10-22-2007 mailed a copy of the first answer.*** *The only difference was that it was a final rejection. All the text was copied from the first answer.)*

(3.4) 09-12-2008 Response to USPTO 08/29/2008

(3.5) Letter to Department of Commerce, sent 09-10-2008

(3.6) USPTO Document from 11-24-2008

(3.7) Reply to the USPTO Document from 11-24-2008, sent 12-05-2008

USPTO Letter from 02-25-2009. Thank you for contacting DoC …

(3.8) 03-02-2009 USPTO Non-Final Rejection *(This is unexpected non-final rejection after USPTO final rejection from 08-29-2008)*

(3.9) 04-02-2009 Response to USPTO non-final rejection from 03-02-2009

(3.10) 05-17-2010 USPTO Final Rejection *(The Second final rejection.)*

(3.11) My response to USPTO document from **5/17/2010** sent 6/2/2010

(3.12) USPTO letter from **11-29-2010.**

(3.13) My response to the USPTO letter from **11-29-2010**

(3.14) 12-02-2010 USPTO Document

(3.15) My response to the USPTO document from 12/02/2010

(3.16) USPTO letter from 12/09/2010

(3.17) My response to the USPTO letter from 12/09/2010

(3.18) USPTO letter from 12/20/2010

(3.19) My response to the USPTO letter from 12/20/2010

(3.20) USPTO letter from 01/06/2011

(3.21) My response to the USPTO letter from 01/06/2011

01-20-2011 USPTO Letter. Thank you for contacting DoC

...

(3.22) Letter to Attorney General and WSJ sent 02/26/20

2.4. REMARKS

2.4.1. Misunderstanding by USPTO of the application essence and the merits

In all the USPTO reviews:

1. All the points of my application are rejected; however, all my drawings were accepted. USPTO reviewer claims that all these provisions stated by Meade in his application number 09/981, 771.

2. USPTO requires me to apply to the patent lawyers for rewriting the application text.

Responding to USPTO in the first point, I have regularly demonstrated by analyzing the Meade application that this is untrue. In this case, I cited in my responses to items of the application and analyzed their statements. I am certain that quite clearly and convincingly proved that the references to the Meade application are improper. The mentioned by the USPTO reviewer materials do not have what the reviewer wrote. There is no text with such meaning; there are no words mentioned by reviewer, there is nothing mentioned by the reviewer.

The Meade application is considering the remote control of all elements of the household. It does not address the issues of information. For example, in the TV the remote control may be done using various devices. For example, you can turn on the TV and change channels by the phone from another country. This does not affect and does not relate the question of getting information from TV antenna or cable.

My application was considering exactly the information provision. It is not discussed in it how to switch on, for example a TV set. The subject is, from where and how to get the program, that is information. It has nothing to do with the Meade application. However, the USPTO does not want to see, or cannot understand or does not wish to take into account this fundamental difference. My explanations are simply ignored.

It is useful to note that the reviewer often rejects my proposals referring to the drawings of the Meade application. At the same time, the reviewers made their own interpretation of the Meade drawings, which do not meet the explanations in the text of the Meade application. However, my pictures, which are accepted by USPTO, are not discussed by reviewer. According to reviewer logic, drawings have priority over application text. According to the USPTO reviewer logic, it is possible to interpret the drawings in any needed way.

I remind that reviewers do copy all the text from one review to the next. In addition, they do not even make out my objections; they ignore them. This is possible only if the reviewers believe that the content of reviews does not matter. All Superior bureaucracy will certainly be on his or her side.

Regarding the second item.

Firstly, it is meaningless to contact a lawyer for editing text, rejected on all points for reason that it is contained in another application. If you intend to save the meaning of alleged proposals, no editing could help to make them different from the mentioned in another application.

Secondly, knowing that my English is in a low level, I applied to professionals with good English for the text editing. I tried to get help from lawyers, but my appeals to lawyers were unsuccessful. Lawyers, by modifying text, distort the meaning of the text, and they insisted on their variant. If I had submitted the text proposed by the lawyer, then it easily would have been rejected by USPTO reviewers, and rejected on the merits.

An application written by fuzzy (florid) legal language allows endless editing and corrections, which lead not only to prolong the time, but to the complete mercy of a lawyer.
In the end, ether you are running out of patience, or running out of money. Surprises the USPTO method for requirements to use lawyers. There is a suspicion in the selflessness of such recommendations.

As examples of legal documents, can serve the guidelines for completing tax returns. A simpler example is the provision on registration for Medicare Part B. There are, instead of a maximum of one page of clearly established text, a multi-page ambiguous document.

2.4.2. Technical Notes

All documents on the USPTO web site are presented as page images and not in a most convenient format. To obtain the document you need to copy each page in a separate file. Further, there are two possible ways.

You can reprint the text of each picture. This is laborious, and especially the time needed for consuming reconciliation of the correctness of the reprinted text.

You can do this automatically, using special software. First, convert the file format of each image. Then the program will recognize the text in the picture. Finally, all the fragments are copied into a single file.

Apparently, USPTO has taken care to create all these difficulties. After all, put the file in a user-friendly format for USPTO is much easier. USPTO originally had such file, and it is in their database. However, it was ordered a special system of recoding. What for? It seems to complicate the user work and the need to resort to lawyers. There may be done reprinting and spending time on other technical issues. This may last for years; lawyers have time, however the money is paid by the client.

I have chosen the second option. I used software, which retains the size and shape of the text, such as italic, or bold. However, there are glitches; for example, I discovered that the number 6 in one place was read as an 8. Maybe I missed such inaccuracies, but they are not essential.

If the reader will need the original text, it is available at USPTO site **http://portal.uspto.gov/external/portal/pair**

The materials are also on my website **http://speculations.us/InIndex/Notebook/History_and_Remarks.htm** where pictures, copied from the site of USPTO, are preserved in its original format. This creates a small inconvenience, one need to call each page separately. However, the use of the USPTO site is significantly uncomfortable.

2.4.3. A remark taken into account.

It should be noted that one requirement of USPTO was taken into account. At the beginning of the application are listed the differences of the presented invention. It turns out that this must be expressed in one sentence. I had several phrases, and it was pointed out as an unacceptable violation of the application form.

I have seen in other applications this section, and it was much of my voluminous. It turns out that other authors have too many phrases (within the meaning of). However, they combine the phrases into one, instead of putting the point they put a semicolon and substituting a capital letter in the following sentence with a lowercase letter, e.g. "**... a. H ...** " is changed to **"... a; h ..."**. I did the same, and the remark was withdrawn.

I recommend the reader to find in a detective a page of text, where is a conversation in which the sides are trying to deceive each other. Combine all phrases it this way and re-read the text. That is where would be the field for ambiguity.

3. MAIN DOCUMENTS

3.1. 10-22-2007 USPTO Non-Final Rejection.
(This is the date of USPTO first reaction.
It passed 2 year and 10 month.*)*

Page 0

UNITED STATES PATENT AND TRADEMARK OFFICE

UNITED STATES DEPARTMENT
OF COMMERCE
United States Patent and
Trademark Office
Address: COMMISSIONER
FOR PATENTS
P.o. Box 1450
Alexandria., Virginia 22313-1450
www.uspto.gov

APPLICATION NO.	FILING DATE
10/905,635	*01/13/2005*

FIRST NAMED INVENTOR	CONFIRMATION NO.
Ilya Kogan	2635

EXAMINER
AKINYEMI, AJIBOLA A

50602 7590

ILYA KOGAN
2573 E. 27TH ST.
BROOKLYN, NY 11235

ART UNIT 2618

MAIL DATE 10/22/2007

Please find below and/or attached an Office communication concerning this application or proceeding.

The time period for reply, if any, is set in the attached communication.

Page 1

Office Action Summary
Application No. 10/905,635

Examiner AJIBOLA AKINYEMI
Applicant(s) KOGAN, ILYA
Art Unit 2618

The MAILING DATE of this communication appears on the cover sheet with the correspondence address –

Period for Reply

A SHORTENED STATUTORY PERIOD FOR REPLY IS SET TO EXPIRE; 1 MONTH(S) OR THIRTY (30) DAYS, WHICHEVER IS LONGER, FROM THE MAILING DATE OF THIS COMMUNICATION.

- Extensions of time may be available under the provisions of 37 CFR 1.136(a). In no event, however, may a reply be timely filed

after SIX (6) MONTHS from the mailing date of this communication.

- If NO period for reply is specified above, the maximum statutory period will apply and will expire SIX (6) MONTHS from the mailing date of this communication.

- Failure to reply within the set or extended period for reply will, by statute, cause the application to become ABANDONED (35 U.S.C. § 133).

Any reply received by the Office later than three months after the mailing date of this communication, even if timely filed, may reduce any earned patent term adjustment. See 37 CFR 1.704(b).

Status

1) **[X]** Responsive to communication(s) filed on 13 *January 2005.*

2a) **[ ]** This action is FINAL. 2b) **[X]** This action is **non-final.**

3) **[ ]** Since this application is in condition for allowance except for formal matters, prosecution as to the merits is closed in accordance with the practice under *Ex Parte Quayle,* 1935 *CD.* 11, 453 O.G. 213.

Disposition of Claims

4) **[X]** Claim(s) *1-10* is/are pending in the application.

4a) Of the above c1aim(s)__is/are withdrawn from consideration.

5) **[ ]** Claim(s)__is/are allowed.

6) **[X]** Claim(s) *1-8 and 10* is/are rejected.

7) **[ ]** Claim(s) 8-9 is/are objected to.

8) **[ ]** Claim(s)__are subject to restriction and/or election requirement.

Application Papers

9) **[ ]** The specification is objected to by the Examiner.

10) **[X]** The drawing(s) filed on 13 *January 2005* is/are: a) **[X]** accepted or b) **[ ]** objected to by the Examiner. Applicant

may not request that any objection to the drawing(s) be held in abeyance. See 37 CFR 1.85(a).

Replacement drawing sheet(s) including the correction is required if the drawing(s) is objected to. See 37 CFR 1.121 (d).

11) [ ] The oath or declaration is objected to by the Examiner. Note the attached Office Action or form PTO-152.

Priority under 35 U.S.C. § 119

12) [ ] Acknowledgment is made of a claim for foreign priority under 35 U.S.C. § 119(a)-(d) or (f).

a) [ ] All b) [ ] Some * c) [ ] None of:

1. [ ] Certified copies of the priority documents have been received.

2. [ ] Certified copies of the priority documents have been received in Application No.__.

3.[ ] Copies of the certified copies of the priority documents have been received in this National Stage application from the International Bureau (PCT Rule 17.2(a».

* See the attached detailed Office action for a list of the certified copies not received.

Attachment(s)

1) **[X]** Notice of References Cited (PTO-892)

2) [ ] Notice of Draftsperson's Patent Drawing Review (PTO-948)

3) [ ] Information Disclosure Statement(s) (PTO/SB/08)
Paper No(s)/Mail Date__.

4) [ ] Interview Summary (PTO-413)
Paper No(s)/Mail Date.__.

5) [ ] Notice of Informal Patent Application

6) [ ] Other:__.

U.S. Patent and Trademark Office

PTOL-326 (Rev. 08-06) Office Action Summary Part of Paper No./Mail Date 20080828

Page 2

Application/Control Number: 10/905,635
Art Unit: 2618

DETAILED ACTION

Claim Objections

1. Claim 8(2·7): unacceptable multiple dependent claim wording. See MPEP § 608.01 (n).

2. Claim 9(1-7): unacceptable multiple dependent claim wording. See MPEP § 608.01 (n).

3. Claim 9 is objected to under 37 CFR 1.75(c) as being in improper form because a multiple dependent claim 8. See MPEP § 608.01(n). Accordingly, the claim 9 is not been further treated on the merits.

Claim Rejections - 35 USC § 112

1. The following is a quotation of the second paragraph of 35 U.S.C. 112:

The specification shall conclude with one or more claims particularly pointing out and distinctly claiming the subject matter, which the applicant regards as his invention.

1. Claims 1-6, 8 are rejected as failing to define the invention in the manner required by 35 U.S.C. 112, second paragraph.

The c1aim(s) are narrative in form and replete with indefinite and functional or operational language. The structure, which goes to make up the device, must be clear1y and positively specified. The structure must be organized and correlated in such a

Page 3

Application/Control Number: *10/905,635*
Art Unit: 2618

manner as to present a complete operative device. The claim(s) must be in one sentence form only. Note the format of the claims in the patent(s) cited.

***Claim Rejections* - 35 *USC* § 102**

2. The following is a quotation of the appropriate paragraphs of 35 U.S.C. 102 that form the basis for the rejections under this section made in this Office action:

A person shall be entitled to a patent unless -

(b) the invention was patented or despaired in a printed publication in this or a foreign country, or in public use, or on sale in this country, more than one year prior the dale of application for patent in the Unites Says.

3. Claim1-2, 5-8, 10 are rejected under 35 U.S.C. 102(b) as being anticipated by Knoble (Pub. No.: US 200210068529A1).

With respect to claim 1:

Knoble teaches which allows with minor changes in the modern cellular phone and without any additional services to eliminate and simplify the usage of many electronics and communication devices of everyday life. (Col. 1, parag.001 0-0011).

With respect to claim 2:

Knoble teaches a method, which allows elimination of any special connection to the Internet such as cable or telephone line (see col.3, parag.0031).

With respect to claim 5:

Knoble teaches a method which allows to use a conventional stationary phone without a phone line and without any additional adapters (see coL1, parag.0010-0011).

With respect to claim 6:

Page 4

Application/Control Number 10/905.635
Art Unit: 2618

Knoble teaches a method that allow to eliminate the necessity of telephone lines which would make it cheaper and elimination of the bill for the telephone line (see col.1, parag.0005, 0010-0011).

With respect to claim 7:

Knoble teaches a method that allows the use of cellular with any standard devices that have a USB input (see col.3, parag.0031).

With respect to claim 8:

Knoble teaches a method in which stationary phones has some function of cellular phone which follows widening usage of cellular phones and necessity for more channel (col. 1, parag. 0010-0011).

With respect to claim 10:

Knoble teaches a method that makes it useful to create a stationary phone with (wireless) input from a hub in addition to other type of phones (see 001.1, parag.0010-0011).

Claim Rejections - 35 *USC* § *103*

4. The following is a quotation of 35 U.S.C. 103(a) which forms the basis for all obviousness rejections set forth in this Office action:

(a) A patent may not be obtained though the invention is not identically disclosed or described as set forth in section 102 of this title, if the differences between the subject matter sought to be patented and the prior art are such that the subject matter as ail would have been obvious at the time the invention was made to a person having ordinary skill in the art to which said subject matter pertains. Patentability shall not be negative by the manner in which the invention was made.

Page 5

Application/Control Number: 10/905,635
Art Unit: 2618

5. The factual inquiries set forth in *Graham* v. *John Deere Co.,* 383 U.S. 1, 148 USPQ 459 (1966), that are applied for establishing a background for determining obviousness under 35 U.S.C. 103(a) are summarized as follows:

1. Determining the scope and contents of the prior art.
2. Ascertaining the differences between the prior art and the claims at issue.
3. Resolving the level of ordinary skill in the pertinent art
4. Considering objective evidence present in the application indicating obviousness or no obviousness.

6. Claim 3 is rejected under 35 U.S.C. 103(a) as being unpatentable over Knoble (Pub. No.: US 200210068529A1) further in view of Watanabe (Pub. No. US 2005/0070327A1).

With respect to claim 3:

Knoble teaches which allows with minor changes in the modern cellular phone and without any additional services to eliminate and simplify the usage of many electronics and communication devices of everyday life. (Col.1, parag.001 0-0011). Knoble differs

from claim invention in that using cell phone to revive TV program and videophone conversation is not taught. Watanabe teaches a method wherein cell phone is been used to receive TV program (see col. 1, parag0005). It would have been obvious to one of ordinary skill in the art at the time the invention was made to have used cell phone that can receive TV program. Modifying Knoble with Watanabe invention will help in elimination of some devices and save money.

Page 6

Application/Control Number: 10/905,635
Art Unit: 2618

7. Claim 4 is rejected under 35 U.S.C. 103(a) as being unpatentable over Knoble (Pub. No.: US 2002J0068529A1) as applied to claim 1 above, and further in view of McZeal (Patent No.: US 676322681).

With respect to claim 4:

Knoble teaches which allows with minor changes in the modern cellular phone and without any additional services to eliminate and simplify the usage of many electronics and. communication devices of everyday life. (Col.1, parag.0010-0011). Knoble differs

from claim invention in that using a cellular phone as a web cam with PC or laptop is not taught. McZeal teaches a portable phone with web cam. It would have been obvious to one of ordinary skill in the art at the time the invention was made to have used a portable phone with a web cam. Modifying Knoble with McZeal invention will help in saving *money* and reduce redundancy.

Conclusion

Any inquiry concerning this communication or earlier communications from the examiner should be directed to Ajibola Akinyemi whose telephone number is (571) 270-1846. The examiner can normally be reached on Monday - Friday (8.30-5pm) Est. If attempts to reach the examiner by telephone are unsuccessful, the examiner's supervisor, LANA LE can be reached on (571) 272-7891. The fax phone number for the organization where this application or proceeding is assigned is 571-273-8300.

Page 7

Application/Control Number: 10/905,635
Art Unit: 2618

Information regarding the status of an application may be obtained from the Patent Application Information Retrieval (PAIR) system. Status information for published applications may be obtained from either Private PAIR or Public PAIR. Status

information for unpublished applications is available through Private PAIR only. For more information about the PAIR system, see http://pair-direct.uspto.gov. Should you have questions on access to the Private PAIR system, contact the Electronic Business Center (ESC) at 866-217-9197 (toll-free). If you would like assistance from a USPTO Customer Service Representative or access to the automated information system, call 800-786-9199 (IN USA OR CANADA) or 571-272-1000.

AA

LANA LE
PRIMARY EXAMINER

3.2. Response to Non-Final Rejection from 10-22-2007.

***(I mailed the response in some 2 weeks, on 11-12-2007.** The reason for such a quick response was no necessity to analyze the USPTO text. It has nothing to do with reality.)*

Page 1

To: Commissioner for Patents,
US Patent and Trademark Office
P.O. Box 1450,
Alexandria, VA 22313 - 1450

From: Ilya Kogan
2573 E 27 St., Brooklyn NY 11235,
kogani@optonline.net, 718/769-8637

Re: Office Action summary to app. No.
10/905635,
art unit 2618 from 10/22/2007, conf. no.
2635,
Examiner AKINYEMI, AJIBOLA

A) GENERAL REMARKS

A1.

1. All your remarks about correspondence to the formal requirement should be fulfilled.

2. You are right by stressing some identity of formulation and identity of content in different applications and patents. This is quite natural, because the authors intend to achieve goals, which are to some extent similar. However:

- Some goals in the applications under consideration are similar only to some extent, they are not identical.

- Even identical goals may be achieved by different means and methods. In the mentioned applications, this **differs principally.**

3. I received your document on October 25. On the envelope, the mailing date is October 22. In the document, the only date is in the lower right corner of page 1. It states – Mail date 200710/04. The difference is three weeks. If the interval would be one month, the difference would be principal.

A2. In the Knoble application (Pub. No.: US 2002/0068529A1 as it is on 10/31/2007)

The goal of the invention is

"[0010] Accordingly, it is an object of the invention to provide a system and method to permit consumers and businesses to avoid redundant telephone service and the costs that are associated with such redundancy.

[0011] In order to achieve the above and other objects of the invention, a method of converting a telephone system that has been connected to the public switched network for cellular usage includes, according to a first aspect of the invention, disconnecting the telephone system from the public switched network; providing an adapter unit that is

Page 2

constructed and arranged to connect to at least one cellular telephone at a first point of connection and to the telephone system at a second point of connection, the adapter including a converter for converting at least one signal from the cellular telephone to at least one signal that is appropriate for use by the telephone system and for converting at least one signal from the telephone system to a signal that is appropriate for use by the cellular telephone; and connecting the adapter unit to the telephone system.."

As it is seen from text and images, this is the only goal: to eliminate telephone lines and associated expenses. I do not mention the phone bill expenses in my application, because I have some doubts whether the enlargement of cell phone expenses may compensate this. In the Knoble, case is the additional cost of the controlling computer, to say nothing about the necessity to learn its operation.

Knoble to achieve the goal proposes **a special device (equivalent to a specialized computer, which has all the features of a typical computer: CPU, keyboard, monitor, and many special features - devices)**. This computerized control device should be placed between the cell phone and traditional phone. Even then, without changes in the cell phone, which Knoble does not mention, it would be impossible to connect to USB.

Today, as well as some 4 years ago, any PC with some well-known external devices may achieve all the goals of Knoble's application. This would be much cheaper, more simple, and faster. However, Knoble's application may be patented. **It is necessary to stress, that this does not interfere with my application.**

A3. In the Watanable application (Pub. No.: US 2005/0070327A1 as it is on 10/31/2007)

The goal of the invention is: *"[0010] A recent cellular phone is designed so as to be folded. The cellular phone comprises a cover portion and a body portion, both being connected to each other by a hinge, and can be held in an open state or in a folded state. A display unit is mounted on the cover portion and a display screen displayed on the display unit can be seen only when the cellular phone is held in the open state.*

When an incoming call is notified, a user uses the cellular phone in the open state for a speaking purpose."

As it is seen from the text and images, this is the only goal - to have the possibility of using the cell phone for e.g. conversations without interrupting watching TV on the cell phone screen. To achieve this goal are proposed some changes in the structure (appearance) of the cell phone, some possible algorithms, and another screen. **It is necessary to stress, that this does not interfere with my application.**

A4. In the Zeal patent (Patent No.: US 6763226B1)

"What I claim as my invention is:

1. A satellite based/tri-frequency cellular wireless apparatus and network for establishing real time instant messaging, Voice Over IP communications, and global

Page

3

unified telecommunications between wireless networks, the public switched telephone network a data network, and the internet, comprising: (a) a built-in Instant Messenger software program capable of automatically connecting to the internet and providing a means for real time two way voice chat, text chat, and video conferencing between two or more wireless devices, and, (b) a external Instant Messenger software program ..."

It is about 100 pages, many pictures of boxes (that tell completely nothing) and flow-charts of algorithms, which are not detailed. As a specialist in electronics, computer hardware and software, I state that an average engineer would create a structure like given in the patent in a couple of days. In addition, anyone may make pictures of dozens of cabinets. It may be patented, but there are great doubts for implementation.

However, the main thing is, this has nothing to do with applications US 2002/0068529A1, US 2005/0070327A1, and US 2006/0154693 (mine).

A5. In the position 7 of "Office Action Summary" is written, *"Modifying Knoble with McZeal invention will help ..."*. This raises a question - Could an invention modify and combine well known and used for years features, if it is proposed a different way of getting those old things? In all the three mentioned publications and one patent it is done largely. **I need to stress, that only Knoble proposed one particular task of the tasks introduced in my application. However, it is proposed to solve it in a completely different way (additional device, which is like a computer and needs a special design) much less convenient, more expensive, and less user friendly. Thousands are working in similar directions, and for last century, there are patented many proposals. Only one goal of my application is similar to Knoble; however, it is solved in a different way.**

A6. In my application (Pub. NO.: US 2006/0154693 as it was on 05/13/2005 and is on 10/31/2007)

[0010] The invention provides a system and method for: [0011] reducing hardware redundancy, e.g. web cam; [0012] reducing additional services as phone cables or (to some extent) TV cable service and internet cable; [0013] possibility of usage of a multi functional device-cellular phone features simultaneously in different stationary devices;
[0014] simplifying maintenance, what is very important for majority of users; [0015] reducing the costs related to all the above. [0016] Wireless electronic system and method based on cellular phone does not require new standards. On the other hand, they allow by changing of scheme and structure of cellular phone and adding new inputs to home information and communication devices to get a completely new quality in usage of multiple electronic devices and phone communication systems. [0017] To achieve the above benefits it is not required any special equipment, adapters, or devices. **It has nothing**

in common with mentioned sources

Page 4

B) ANSWERS TO SPECIFIC POSITIONS

B1. Answers to your pos. 3 (page 3)

To "With respect to claim 1". There is no such expression in Knoble application "**additional services to eliminate and simplify the usage of many electronic and communication devices of everyday life"** in Col. 1, parag. 0010-0011.

To "With respect to claim 2". In col. 3 parag 0031 it is mentioned, that a computer (device 16) can perform different programs. **It is not proposed to eliminate something it is a general remark.** Related to Knoble case, it is wrong.

To "With respect to claim 5". *"[0011] ... disconnecting the telephone system from the public switched network; providing an **adapter** unit that is constructed and arranged ... use by the cellular telephone; and connecting the **adapter** unit to the telephone system.."* In col. 3 parag 0031 it is mentioned, that a computer (device 16) can perform different programs. **It is not proposed to eliminate something.** It is **not written** without any additional adapter. **If it is possible to do without an additional adapter, then what is the goal of Knoble application?** It is written by Knoble about eliminating expenses (a very doubtful question in his case), however, with different means and methods.

To "With respect to claim 7". In col. 3 parag 0031 it is mentioned, that a computer (device 16) can have USB connections. **It is not proposed to eliminate something it is a general remark.** The remark is related, according to pos. 0031 only to Internet connection and needs a special device (universal computer with some additional devises). It is impossible to get Internet in his case.

To "With respect to claim 8". In the col. 1, parag. 0010-0011, there is no such thought directly or indirectly.

To "With respect to claim 10". In the col. 1, parag. 0010-0011, there is no such thought directly or indirectly. The word **HUB** is not present in the Knoble application (as on 10/31/2007).

To your pos. 6 (page 5), with respect to claim 3 and pos. 7 (page 6) with respect to claim 4. Knoble does not mention **TV** in 0010 or 0011; Watanabe speaks about TV in completely different aspect. McZeal has different goals. Modifying and combining different applications and patent is possible to achieve everything.

Page 5

CONCLUSION

Analysis of your text and my answers leads to the conclusion, that you have Knoble application text that principally differs from one in Pub. No.: US 2002/0068529A1 as it is on 10/31/2007. Knoble teaches, "... ***it is an object of the invention to provide a system and method to permit consumers and businesses to avoid redundant telephone service and the costs that are associated with such redundancy",*** this is the only goal Knoble teaches. This is proposed to do with an intermediate very complex additional device. This device accordingly to Knoble is like a computer with many additional special devices. I do not mention about eliminating the cost of the phone line - the additional costs of cell phones may be greater. **All else, what is written in your document as Knoble teaches, has nothing to do with officially published Knoble application. The Knoble application has no such words. The application has no such proposals or hints, in the smallest degree.**

The problem is either I should make my application to correspond to some formal rules, or in some other application or patent, this already exists and my application is garbage. The latter may happen, however it has nothing to do with the Knoble and Watanabe applications and McZeal patent. On the other hand, I believe that if one (answering to patent office remarks) principally changes his original application, his completely different new one cannot be in force.

ATTACHMENT

To this document is attached grammatically edited application. The minor grammatical edit was made in such a way, that it would escape your general objections. E.g., several phrases were combined into one with the help of semicolons instead of periods. The references to multiple cases were eliminated.

There is no problem of including algorithm flowcharts. However, this may be treated as changing the subject. On the other hand, the flowcharts given by Watanabe or McZeal have nothing original and specific (as McZeal cabinets) and do not add any new feature to their proposals. If this is required, I have the algorithms and flowcharts and can add them.

Sincerely Ilya Kogan

November 12, 2007

3.3. 08-29-2008 USPTO Final Rejection.
(In 9 month, USPTO on 10-22-2007 mailed a copy of the first answer. *The only difference was that it was a final rejection. All the text was copied from the first answer.)*

Page 0

UNITED STATES PATENT AND TRADEMARK OFFICE

UNITED STATES DEPARTMENT OF COMMERCE
United States Patent and Trademark Office
Address: COMMISSIONER FOR PATENTS
P.o. Box 1450
Alexandria., Virginia 22313-1450
www.uspto.gov

APPLICATION NO.
10/905,635

FILING DATE
01/13/2005

FIRST NAMED INVENTOR
Ilya Kogan

CONFIRMATION NO.
2635

EXAMINER
AKINYEMI, AJIBOLA A
50602 7590

ILYA KOGAN
2573 E. 27TH ST.
BROOKLYN, NY 11235

ART UNIT 2618

MAIL DATE 08/29/2008

Please find below and/or attached an Office communication concerning this application or proceeding.

The time period for reply, if any, is set in the attached communication.

Page 1

Office Action Summary

Application No. 10/905,635

Examiner AJIBOLA AKINYEMI

Applicant(s) KOGAN, ILYA

Art Unit 2618

The MAILING DATE of this communication appears on the cover sheet with the correspondence address –

Period for Reply

A SHORTENED STATUTORY PERIOD FOR REPLY IS SET TO EXPIRE 1 MONTH(S) OR THIRTY (30) DAYS, WHICHEVER IS LONGER, FROM THE MAILING DATE OF THIS COMMUNICATION.

- Extensions of time may be available under the provisions of 37 CFR 1.136(a). In no event, however, may reply be timely filed

after SIX (6) MONTHS from the mailing date of this communication.

- If NO period for reply is specified above, the maximum statutory period will apply and will expire SIX (6) MONTHS from the mailing date of this communication.

- Failure to reply within the set or extended period for reply will, by statute, cause the application to become ABANDONED (35 U.S.C. § 133).

Any reply received by the Office later than three months after the mailing date of this communication, even if timely filed, may reduce any earned patent term adjustment. See 37 CFR 1.704(b).

Status

1) **[X]** Responsive to communication(s) filed on 16 *November 2007.*

2a) **[X]** This action is **FINAL**. 2b) **[}** This action is non-final.

3) **[ ]** Since this application is in condition for allowance except for formal matters, prosecution as to the merits is closed in accordance with the practice under *Ex Parte Quayle,* 1935 *CD.* 11, 453 O.G. 213.

Disposition of Claims

4) **[X]** Claim(s) *1-10* is/are pending in the application.

4a) Of the above c1aim(s)__is/are withdrawn from consideration.

5) **[ ]** Claim(s)__is/are allowed.

6) **[X]** Claim(s) ***1-10* is/are rejected**.

7) **[ ]** Claim(s)__is/are objected to.

8) **[ ]** Claim(s)__are subject to restriction and/or election requirement.

Application Papers

9) **[ ]** The specification is objected to by the Examiner.

10) **[X]** The drawing(s) filed on 13 *October 2005* is/are: a) **[X] accepted** or b) **[ ]** objected to by the Examiner. Applicant may not request that any objection to the drawing(s) be held in abeyance. See 37 CFR 1.85(a).

Replacement drawing sheet(s) including the correction is required if the drawing(s) is objected to. See 37 CFR 1.121 (d).

11) **[ ]** The oath or declaration is objected to by the Examiner. Note the attached Office Action or form PTO-152.

Priority under 35 U.S.C. § 119

12) [ ] Acknowledgment is made of a claim for foreign priority under 35 U.S.C. § 119(a)-(d) or (f).

a) [ ] All b) [ ] Some * c) [ ] None of:

1. [ ] Certified copies of the priority documents have been received.

2. [ ] Certified copies of the priority documents have been received in Application No.__.

3.[ ] Copies of the certified copies of the priority documents have been received in this National Stage application from the International Bureau (PCT Rule 17.2(a».

* See the attached detailed Office action for a list of the certified copies not received.

Attachment(s)

1) **[X]** Notice of References Cited (PTO-892)

2) [ ] Notice of Draftsperson's Patent Drawing Review (PTO-948)

3) [ ] Information Disclosure Statement(s) (PTO/SB/08)
Paper No(s)/Mail Date__.

4) [ ] Interview Summary (PTO-413)
Paper No(s)/Mail Date.__.

5) [ ] Notice of Informal Patent Application

6) [ ] Other:__.

U.S. Patent and Trademark Office

PTOL-326 (Rev. 08-06) Office Action Summary Part of Paper No./Mail Date 20080828

Page 2

Application/Control Number: 10/905,635
Art Unit: 2618

Claim Rejections* - 35 *USC* § *102

1. The following is a quotation of the appropriate paragraphs of 35 U.S.C. 102 that form the basis for the rejections under this section made in this Office action:

A person shall be entitled to a patent unless -

(b) the invention was patented or described in a printed publication in this or a foreign country, in public use, or on sale in this country, more than one year prior to the date of application for patent in the United States.

2. Claim1-2, 5-8, 10 are rejected under 35 U.S.C. 102(b) as being anticipated by Knoble (Pub. No.: US 2002/0068529A1).

With respect to claim 1:

Knoble teaches a method which allows with minor changes in the modern cellular phone and without any additional services to eliminate and simplify the usage of many electronics and communication devices of everyday life. (Col. 1, parag.001 0-0011).

With respect to claim 2:

Knoble teaches a method which allows elimination of any special connection to the Internet such as cable or telephone line (see col.3, parag.0031).

With respect to claim 5:

Knoble teaches a method which allows to use a conventional stationary phone without a phone line and without any additional adapters (see col. 1, parag.001 0-0011).

With respect to claim 6:

Page 3

Application/Control Number: 10/905,635
Art Unit: 2618

Knoble teaches a method that allow to eliminate the necessity of telephone lines which would make it cheaper and elimination of the bill for the telephone line (see col. 1, parag.0005, 0010-0011).

With respect to claim 7:

Knoble teaches a method that allows the use of cellular with any standard devices that have a USB input (see col.3, parag.0031).

With respect to claim 8:
Knoble teaches a method in which stationary phones has some function of cellular phone which follows widening usage of cellular phones and necessity for more channel
(col.1, parag. 0010-0011).

With respect to claim 10:

Knoble teaches a method that make it useful to create a stationary phone with (wireless) input from a hub in addition to other type of phones (see col. 1, parag.001 0- 0011).

Claim Rejections - 35 USC § 103

3. The following is a quotation of 35 U.S.C. 103(a) which forms the basis for all obviousness rejections set forth in this Office action:

(a) A patent may not be obtained though the invention is not identically disclosed or described as set forth in section 102 of this title, if the differences between the subject matter sought to be patented and the prior art are such that the subject matter as a whole would have been obvious at the time the invention was made to a person having ordinary skill in the art to which said subject matter pertains. Patentability shall not be negatived by the manner in which the invention was made.

Page 4

Application/Control Number: 10/905,635
Art Unit: 2618

4. The factual inquiries set forth in *Graham* v. *John Deere* Co., 383 U.S. 1, 148 USPQ 459 (1966), that are applied for establishing a background for determining obviousness under 35 U.S.C. 103(a) are summarized as follows:

1. Determining the scope and contents of the prior art.

2. Ascertaining the differences between the prior art and the claims at issue.

3. Resolving the level of ordinary skill in the pertinent art.

4. Considering objective evidence present in the application indicating obviousness or no obviousness.

5. Claim 3 is rejected under 35 U.S.C. 103(a) as being unpatentable over Knoble (Pub. No.: US 2002/0068529A1) further in view of Watanabe (Pub. No. US 2005/0070327A1).

With respect to claim 3:

Knoble teaches which allows with minor changes in the modern cellular phone and without any additional services to eliminate and simplify the usage of many electronics and communication devices of everyday life. (Col.1, parag.001 0-0011). Knoble differs

from claim invention in that using cell phone to revive TV program and videophone conversation is not taught. Watanabe teaches a method wherein cell phone is been used to receive TV program (see col. 1, parag0005). It would have been obvious to one of ordinary skill in the art at the time the invention was made to have used cell phone that can receive TV program. Modifying Knoble with Watanabe invention will help in elimination of some devices and save money.

Page 5

Application/Control Number: 10/905,635
Art Unit: 2618

6. Claim 4 is rejected under 35 U.S.C. 103(a) as being unpatentable over Knoble (Pub. No.: US 2002/0068529A1) as applied to claim1 above, and further in view of McZeal (Patent No.: US 676322681).

With respect to claim 4:

Knoble teaches which allows with minor changes in the modern cellular phone and without any additional services to eliminate and simplify the usage of many electronics and communication devices of everyday life. (Col.1, parag.001 0-0011). Knoble differs from claim invention in that using a cellular phone as a web cam with PC or laptop is not taught. McZeal teaches a portable phone with web cam. It would have been obvious to one of ordinary skill in the art at the time the invention was made to have used a portable phone with a web cam. Modifying Knoble with McZeal invention will help in saving money and reduce redundancy.

With respect to claim 9:

McZeal teaches a method that allows using the cellular phone as an input to a hub for transferring signal to different device (fig.5, item 13A).

Response to Arguments

7. Applicant should submit an argument under the heading "Remarks" pointing out disagreements with the examiner's contentions. Applicant must also discuss the references applied against the claims, explaining how the claims avoid the references or distinguish from them.

Page 6

Application/Control Number: 10/905,635
Art Unit: 2618

Conclusion

8. **THIS ACTION IS MADE FINAL.** Applicant is reminded of the extension of time policy as set forth in 37 CFR 1.136(a).

A shortened statutory period for reply to this final action is set to expire THREE MONTHS from the mailing date of this action. In the event a first reply is filed within TWO MONTHS of the mailing date of this final action and the advisory action is not mailed until after the end of the THREE-MONTH shortened statutory period, then the shortened statutory period will expire on the date the advisory action is mailed, and any extension fee pursuant to 37 CFR 1.136(a) will be calculated from the mailing date of the advisory action. In no event, however, will the statutory period for reply expire later than SIX MONTHS from the mailing date of this final action.

Any inquiry concerning this communication or earlier communications from the examiner should be directed to AJIBOLA AKINYEMI whose telephone number is (571)270-1846. The examiner can normally be reached on Monday- Friday (8.30-5pm) Est.

If attempts to reach the examiner by telephone are unsuccessful, the examiner's supervisor, YUWEN PAN can be reached on (571) 272-7855. The fax phone number for the organization where this application or proceeding is assigned is 571-273-8300.

Page

7

Application/Control Number: 10/905,635
Art Unit: 2618

Information regarding the status of an application may be obtained from the Patent Application Information Retrieval (PAIR) system. Status information for published applications may be obtained from either Private PAIR or Public PAIR.

Status information for unpublished applications is available through Private PAIR only. For more information about the PAIR system, see http://pair-direct.uspto.gov. Should you have questions on access to the Private PAIR system, contact the Electronic Business Center (EBC) at 866-217-9197 (toll-free). If you would like assistance from a USPTO Customer Service Representative or access to the automated information system, call 800-786-9199 (IN USA OR CANADA) or 571-272-1000.

AA
/Yuwen Pan/

Primary Examiner, Art Unit 2618

3.4. 09-12-2008 Response to USPTO 08/29/2008

Page 1

To: Commissioner for Patents,
US Patent and Trademark Office
P.O. Box 1450,
Alexandria, VA 22313 - 1450

From: Ilya Kogan
2573 E 27 St., Brooklyn NY 11235,
kogani@optonline.net, 718/769-8637

Re: Office Action summary to app. No.
10/905635,
Art unit 2618
From 08/29/2008, conf. no. 2635,
Examiner AKINYEMI, AJIBOLA

ANSWERS TO MAIN POSITIONS

1. You are right by stressing some identity of formulation and identity of content in different applications and patents. This is quite natural, because the authors intend to achieve goals, which are to some extent similar. However:

- Some goals in the applications under consideration may be similar only to some extent, but they are not identical. In addition, I did not find the identity, which you are writing about, even in a single position.

- Even identical goals may be achieved by different means and methods. In the mentioned in your document applications, **the goals and solutions differ principally.**

2. On page 2 in pos. 2 is written, **"With respect to claim 1:** ***Knoble teaches a method which allows with minor changes in the modern cellular phone and without any additional services to eliminate and simplify the usage of many electronics and communication devices of everyday life. (Col. 1, parag. 0010-0011)"***

There is no such expression in Knoble application "additional services to eliminate and simplify the usage of many electronic and communication devices of everyday life" in Col. 1, parag. 0010 - 0011.

In the Knoble application (Pub. No.: US 2002/0068529A1 as it was published on June 6 2002 and must be now). The goal of the invention is

"[0010] Accordingly, it is an object of the invention to provide a system and method to permit consumers and businesses to avoid redundant telephone service and the costs that are associated with such redundancy.

[0011] In order to achieve the above and other objects of the invention, a method of converting a telephone system that has been connected to the public switched network for cellular usage includes, according to a first aspect of the invention, disconnecting the

Page 2

telephone system from the public switched network; providing an adapter unit that is constructed and arranged to connect to at least one cellular telephone at a first point of connection and to the telephone system at a second point of connection, the adapter including a converter for converting at least one signal from the cellular telephone to at least one signal that is appropriate for use by the telephone system and for converting at least one signal from the telephone system to a signal that is appropriate for use by the cellular telephone; and connecting the adapter unit to the telephone system.."

As it is seen from text and images, this is the only goal: to eliminate telephone lines and associated expenses. I do not mention the phone bill expenses in my application, because I have some doubts whether the enlargement of cell phone expenses may compensate this. In the Knoble case is the additional cost of the controlling computer, to say nothing about the necessity to learn its operation.

To achieve the goal Knoble proposes **a special device (equivalent to a specialized computer, which has all the features of a typical computer: CPU, keyboard, monitor, and many special features - devices)**. This computerized control device should be placed between the cell phone and traditional phone. **Even then, without changes in the cell phone, which Knoble does not mention, it would be impossible to connect to USB.**

3. On page 2 in pos 2 is written,"**With respect to claim 2:** ***Knoble teaches a method which allows elimination of any special connection to the Internet such as cable or telephone line (see col.3, parag.0031)."***

In col. 3 parag 0031 it is mentioned, that a computer (device 16) can perform different programs. **It is not proposed to eliminate something it is a general remark.** Related to Knoble case, it is wrong.

In the Knoble application parag. 0031 (Pub. No.: US 2002/0068529A1 as it was on June 6 2002 and must be now).

[0031] Many cellular service providers are now offering Internet access via cellular telephone. In order to capitalize on this service, apparatus 16 could further be constructed and arranged so as to be able to convert this data to and from a protocol that would be understandable by a personal computer or Internet appliance. Apparatus 16 could be provided with a connector for this purpose, which could be an ethernet port or a USB port that could easily be connected to a personal computer.

It is necessary to stress, that this does not interfere with my application.

Ones more, to achieve the goal Knoble proposes **a special device (equivalent to a specialized computer, which has all the features of a typical computer: CPU, keyboard, monitor, and many special features - devices)**. This computerized control device should be placed between the cell phone and traditional phone. Even then, without

Page 3

changes in the cell phone, which Knoble does not mention, it would be impossible to connect to USB. **After changing the cell phone, it may be done with any computer.** In addition, today, as well as some 6 years ago, any PC with some well-known external devices may achieve all the goals of the Knoble application. This would be much cheaper, more simple, and faster.

4. On page 2 in pos. 2 is written, **"With respect to claim 5**: ***Knoble teaches a method which allows to use a conventional stationary phone without a phone line and without any additional adapters (see col. 1, parag.0010-0011)."***

Knoble writes, *"... disconnecting the telephone system from the public switched network; providing an* ***adapter*** *unit that is constructed and arranged ... use by the cellular telephone; and connecting the* ***adapter*** *unit to the telephone system.."* In col. 3 parag 0031 it is mentioned, that a computer (device 16) can perform different programs. **It is not proposed to eliminate something.** It is **not written** without any additional adapter. **If it is possible to do without an additional adapter, then what is the goal of Knoble application?**

There is an additional device as complex as a computer. This is repeated many times in text and shown in the pictures. **In the Knoble application (Pub. No.: US 2002/0068529A1 as it was on June 6 2002 and must be now)**. See above copy of parag. 0010-0011.

5. On pages 2-3 in pos. 2 is written, **"With respect to claim 6**: ***Knoble teaches a method that allow to eliminate the necessity of telephone lines which would make it cheaper and elimination of the bill for the telephone line (see col. 1, parag.0005, 0010-0011)."***

In the Knoble application (Pub. No.: US 2002/0068529A1 as it was on June 6 2002 and must be now). See above the parag. 0010-0011.

- The elimination of telephone lines may be done by many different methods. My proposal has nothing to do with Knoble one.

- As it is written above, I do not mention the phone bill expenses in my application, because I have some doubts whether the enlargement of cell phone expenses may compensate this. In the way it is done in the Knoble application, the bill for sure would be greater.

6. On page 3 in pos 2 is written, **"With respect to claim 7:** ***Knoble teaches a method that allows the use of cellular with any standard devices that have a USB input (see col.3, parag.0031)."***

Page 4

In col. 3 parag 0031 it is mentioned, that a computer (device 16) can perform different programs. **It is not proposed to eliminate something it is a general remark.** Related to Knoble case, it is wrong.

The Knoble application parag. 0031 (Pub. No.: US 2002/0068529A1 as it was on June 6 2002 and must be now). It is copied above.

In col. 3 parag 0031 it is mentioned, that a computer (device 16) can have USB connections. Every computer has USB connections. **It is not proposed to eliminate something it is a general remark.** The remark is related, according to pos. 0031 only to Internet connection and it is needed a special device (a universal computer with some additional devises). It is impossible to get Internet in his case without those special devices.

7. On page 3 in pos. 2 is written, **"With respect to claim 8***: Knoble teaches a method in which stationary phones has some function of cellular phone which follows widening usage of cellular phones and necessity for more channel (col.1, parag. 0010-0011)."*

In the Knoble application (Pub. No.: US 2002/0068529A1 as it was on June 6 2002 and must be now). See above the parag. 0010-0011.

In the col. 1, parag. 0010-0011, there is no such thought directly or indirectly.

8. On page 3 in pos. 2 is written, **"With respect to claim 10***: Knoble teaches a method that make it useful to create a stationary phone with (wireless) input from a hub in addition to other type of phones (see col. 1, parag.0010-0011)."*

In the Knoble application (Pub. No.: US 2002/0068529A1 as it was on June 6 2002 and must be now). See above the parag. 0010-0011.

In the col. 1, parag. 0010-0011, there is no such thought directly or indirectly. The word **HUB** is not present in the Knoble application.

9. Due to completely baseless argumentation, what is shown in this document, the pos 3 on page 3 and position 4 on page 4 cannot be used (even mentioned) in this case.

10. On page 4 in pos. 5 is written, **"With respect to claim 3,** ***Knoble teaches which allows with minor changes in the modern cellular phone and without any additional services to eliminate and simplify the usage of many electronics and communication devices of everyday life. (Col.1, parag.0010-0011). Knoble differs from claim invention in that using cell phone to revive TV program and videophone conversation is not taught. Watanabe teaches a method wherein cell phone is been used to receive TV program (see***

Page 5

col. 1, parag0005). It would have been obvious to one of ordinary skill in the art at the time the invention was made to have used cell phone that can receive TV program.

Modifying Knoble with Watanabe invention will help in elimination of some devices and save money"

In the Watanabe application (Pub. No.: US 2005/0070327A1), the goal of the invention is: *"[0010] A recent cellular phone is designed so as to be folded. The cellular phone comprises a cover portion and a body portion, both being connected to each other by a hinge, and can be held in an open state or in a folded state. A display unit is mounted on the cover portion and a display screen displayed on the display unit can be seen only when the cellular phone is held in the open state. When an incoming call is notified, a user uses the cellular phone in the open state for a speaking purpose."*

As it is seen from the text and images, this is the only goal - to have the possibility of using the cell phone for e.g. conversations without interrupting watching TV on the cell phone screen. To achieve this goal are proposed some changes in the structure (appearance) of the cell phone, some possible algorithms, and another screen. **It is necessary to stress, that this does not interfere with my application. To say nothing, that combination of two patents may be patented as well.**

11. On page 5 in pos. 6 is written, **"With respect to claim 3,** ***Knoble teaches which allows with minor changes in the modern cellular phone and without any additional services to eliminate and simplify the usage of many electronics and communication devices of everyday life. (Col.1, parag.0010-0011). Knoble differs from claim invention in that using cell phone to revive TV program and videophone conversation is not taught. Watanabe teaches a method wherein cell phone is been used to receive TV program (see col. 1, parag0005). It would have been obvious to one of ordinary skill in the art at the time the invention was made to have used cell phone that can receive TV program. Modifying Knoble with Watanabe invention will help in elimination of some devices and save money".***

Near the same is repeated on page 6 in pos. 7, **"With respect to claim 4,** ***Knoble teaches which allows with minor changes in the modern cellular phone and without any additional services to eliminate and simplify the usage of many electronics and communication devices of everyday life. (Col.1, parag.0010-0011). Knoble differs from claim invention in that using a cellular phone as a web cam with PC or laptop is not taught. McZeal teaches a portable phone with web cam. It would have been obvious to one of ordinary skill in the art at the time the invention was made to have used a portable phone with a web cam. Modifying Knoble with McZeal invention will help in saving money and reduce redundancy".***

Page 6

In the Zeal patent (Patent No.: US 6763226B1), *"What I claim as my invention is:*

1. A satellite based/tri-frequency cellular wireless apparatus and network for establishing real time instant messaging, Voice Over IP communications, and global unified telecommunications between wireless networks, the public switched telephone network a data network, and the internet, comprising: (a) a built-in Instant Messenger software program capable of automatically connecting to the internet and providing a means for real time two way voice chat, text chat, and video conferencing between two or more wireless devices, and, (b) a external Instant Messenger software program ..."

The patent is about 100 pages, many pictures of boxes (that tell completely nothing) and flow-charts of algorithms, which are not detailed. As a specialist in electronics, computer hardware and software, I state that an average engineer would create a structure as given in the patent in a couple of days. In addition, anyone may make pictures of dozens of different cabinets. It may be patented, but there are great doubts for implementation. **However, the main thing is, this has nothing to do with my application US 2006/0154693.**

Knoble does not mention **TV** in 0010 or 0011; Watanabe speaks about TV in completely different aspect. McZeal has different goals. In addition, modifying and combining different applications and patent is possible to get everything.

The phrase, *"Modifying Knoble with McZeal invention will help ..."* This raises a question - Could an invention modify and combine well known and used for years features, if it is proposed a different way of getting those old things? **I need to stress, that only Knoble proposed one particular task, which is introduced in my application. However, Knoble proposed to solve it in a completely different way (additional device, which is like a computer, what needs a special design and may be patented separately) much less convenient, more expensive, and less user friendly. Thousands are working in similar directions, and for last century, there are patented many proposals. Only one goal of my application is to some extent**

similar to Knoble; however, it is solved in a completely different way.

12. On page 5 in pos. 6 is written, **"With respect to claim 9,** ***McZeal teaches a method that allows using the cellular phone as an input to a hub for transferring signal to different device (fig.5, item 13A)".*** **THIS IS THE ONLY PHRASE NOT COPIED FROM THE DOCUMENT SENT TO ME BY USPTO 10/22/2007 (My reply to it was sent 11/12/2007).**

The reference is not accurate; it refers to a figure, not to the text. I do not propose to use hubs; I propose to connect the cellular phone directly to the stationary phone without an intermediate hub or special and expensive computers.

Page 7

CONCLUSION

1. In my answer dated 11/12/2007, I wrote:

Analysis of your text and my answers leads to the conclusion, that you have Knoble application text that principally differs from one in Pub. No.: US 2002/0068529A1 as it is published by USPTO. Knoble teaches, "... ***it is an object of the invention to provide a system and method to permit consumers and businesses to avoid redundant telephone service and the costs that are associated with such redundancy",*** this is the only goal Knoble teaches. This is proposed to do with an intermediate very complex additional device. This device accordingly to Knoble is like a universal computer with many additional special devices. I do not mention about eliminating the cost of the phone line – the additional costs of cell phones may be greater. **All else, what is written in your document as Knoble teaches, has nothing to do with officially published Knoble application. The Knoble application has no such words. The application has no such proposals or hints, in the smallest degree.**

The problem is either I should make my application to correspond to some formal rules, or in some other application or patent, this already exists and my application is garbage. The latter may happen, however it has nothing to do with the Knoble and Watanabe applications or McZeal patent. It has nothing to do with analysis done by USPTO.

2. On 08/29/2008 was sent the next document. The new document is a copy of all the points from the old one. Thus, that for USPTO it takes about a year to copy several pages. The new material is only conclusion, that the rejection is final. On the other hand, it was given three month for reply. I understand this as a formality, which is needed to reject an application without any reason.

If, e.g., it would be written, that some one decided to apply for a patent with a copy of my application, and that is why my application must be rejected, it would be understandable. It is possible to invent a dozen more such reasons, but the current reason I cannot understand it is the ugliest.

However, my current reply was written with analysis of the USPTO letter. This is done not because I have any chance that it would be taken into account; it is done to show once more the behavior of USPTO. From now on, my main goal is not to get an approval for my application. I want some punishment for people, who allow such behavior. Due to this, I do not expect any objective solution from USPTO and mail a copy with a cover letter to U.S. Department of Commerce Office of Inspector General.

Sincerely Ilya Kogan
September 10, 2008

3.5. Letter to Department of Commerce, sent 09-10-2008

To: Inspector General of the U.S. Department of Commerce U.S. Department of Commerce
Office of Inspector General
1401 Constitution Avenue, N.W. Room 7898C
Washington, D.C. 20230

From: Ilya Kogan
2573 E 27 St., Brooklyn NY 11235,
kogani@optonline.net, 718/769-8637

Re: Office Action Summaries to app. No. 10/905635, art unit 2618 from 08/29/2008, and from 10/22/2007 conf. no. 2635;

Dear Sir, Madam,

On 01/13/2005, I made an application for a patent.

On 10/22/2007, it was sent the first "Office Action Summary". It was marked as non-final, and it was given three month for an answer

On 08/29/2008, it was sent the second "Office Action Summary". It was marked as **FINAL,** and it was given three month for an answer.

The first Office Action Summary rejected all my claims. It was written that in some another application there was the same. It may happen. However, when I read the mentioned application, I did not find this. There were not words or even meaning, which was written in the USPTO document. I wrote an answer (11/12/2007), in which it was shown. There were also some remarks about the form of the document, which I corrected.

In about ten months, I received the second Office Action Summary with final rejection for all my claims. When I read it, I find out that it is a copy (exact copy!) of the first one, without the remarks about the form of the application. If they decided to reject, the form does not matter. I understand that it is useless to apply to USPTO for any reasonable discussion. Even so, I write and sent to USPTO a solid background, which shows that all their remarks have nothing to do with reality. My answer is attached to this letter.

On the other hand, I decided to apply for justice. **If I write to the wrong place, please supply me with a correct one.**

Below is the conclusion from my letter, which you can find in the attachment as well.

CONCLUSION from the letter to USPTO from 08/29/2008

1. In my answer dated 11/12/2007, I wrote, **Analysis of your text and my answers leads to the conclusion, that you have Knoble application text that principally differs from one in Pub. No.: US 2002/0068529A1 as it is published by USPTO. Knoble teaches, "*... it is an object of the invention to provide a system and method to permit consumers and businesses to avoid redundant telephone service and the costs that are associated with such redundancy*",** this is the only goal Knoble teaches. This is proposed to do with an intermediate very complex additional device. This device accordingly to Knoble is like a universal computer with many additional special devices. I do not mention about eliminating the cost of the phone line - the additional costs of cell phones may be greater. **All else, what is written in your document as Knoble teaches, has nothing to do with officially published Knoble application. The Knoble application has no such words. The application has no such proposals or hints, in the smallest degree.**

The problem is either I should make my application to correspond to some formal rules, or in some other application or patent, this already exists and my application is garbage. The latter may happen, however it has nothing to do with the Knoble and Watanabe applications or McZeal patent. It has nothing to do with analysis done by USPTO.

2. On 08/29/2008 was sent the next document. The new document is a copy of all the points from the old one. Thus, that for USPTO it takes about a year to copy several pages. The new material is only conclusion, that the rejection is final. On the other hand, it was given three month for reply. I understand this as a formality, which is needed to reject an application without any reason.

If, e.g., it would be written, that some one decided to apply for a patent with a copy of my application, and that is why my application must be rejected, it would be understandable. It is possible to invent a dozen more such reasons, but the current reason I cannot understand it is the ugliest.

However, my current reply was written with analysis of the USPTO letter. This is done not because I have any chance that it would be taken into account; it is done to show once more the behavior of USPTO. From now on, my main goal is not to get an approval for my application. I want some punishment for people, who allow such behavior. Due to this, I do not expect any objective solution from USPTO and mail a copy with a cover letter to U.S. Department of Commerce Office of Inspector General.

ATTACHMENT Answer to Office Action summary to app. No. 10/905635, from 10/22/2007 (7 pages)

Sincerely Ilya Kogan

September 10, 2008

3.6. USPTO Document from 11-24-2008

This document contains 4 pages

-- Page 1

UNITED STATES PATENT AND TRADEMARK OFFICE

UNITED STATES DEPARTMENT OF COMMERCE
United States Patent and Trademark Office
Address: COMMISSIONER FOR PATENTS
P.o. Box 1450
Alexandria., Virginia 22313-1450
www.uspto.gov

APPLICATION NO. 10/905,635

FILING DATE *01/13/2005*

FIRST NAMED INVENTOR Ilya Kogan

CONFIRMATION NO. 2635

EXAMINER
AKINYEMI, AJIBOLA A
50602 7590

ILYA KOGAN
2573 E. 27TH ST.
BROOKLYN, NY 11235

ART UNIT 2618

MAIL DATE 11/24/2008

Please find below and/or attached an Office communication concerning this application or proceeding.

The time period for reply, if any, is set in the attached communication.

-- Page 2

Advisory Action
Before the Filing of an Appeal Brief
Application No. *10/905,635*
Examiner AJIBOLA AKINYEMI
Applicant(s) KOGAN, ILYA
Art Unit 2618

The MAILING DATE of this communication appears on the* cover *sheet with the* correspondence *address

THE REPLY FILED 12 September 2008 FAILS TO PLACE THIS APPLICATION IN CONDITION FOR ALLOWANCE.

1. **[X]** The reply was filed after a final rejection, but prior to or on the same day as filing a Notice of Appeal. To avoid abandonment of this application, applicant must timely file one of the following replies: (1) an amendment, affidavit, or other evidence, which places the application in condition for allowance; (2) a Notice of Appeal (with appeal fee) in compliance with 37 CFR 41.31; or (3) a Request for Continued Examination (RCE) in compliance with 37 CFR 1.114. The reply must be filed within one of the following time periods:

a) **[ ]** The period for reply expires____ months from the mailing date of the final rejection.

b) **[X]** The period for reply expires on: (1) the mailing date of this Advisory Action, or

(2) The date set for this the final rejection. Whichever is later. In no event, however, will the statutory period for reply expire later than SIX MONTHS from the mailing date at the final rejection Examiner Note: If boll 1 is checked, check either box (a) or (a) ONLY CHECK BOX (b} WHEN THE FIRST REPLY WAS FILED WITHIN TWO MONTHS OF THE FINAL REJECTION, See MPEP 7O6.07(t).

Extensions or time may be obtained under 37 CFR 1.136(3). The date on which the petition under 37 CFR 1.136(3) and the appropriate extension fee have been filed is the date for purposes of determining the period or extension and the corresponding amount of the fee. The appropriate extension fee

under 37 CFR 1 17{a) is calculated from: (1) the expiration date of the shortened statutory period for reply originally set in the final Office action: or (2) as set on in (b) above, if checked. Any reply received by the Office tater than three months after the mailing *date* of the final rejection, even if timely filed, may reduce any patent term adjustment. See 37 CFR 1704(b}.

NOTICE OF APPEAL

2. [ ] The Notice of Appeal was flied on__. A brief in compliance with 37 CFR 41.37 must be filed within two months of the date of

filling the Notice of Appeal (37 CFR 41.37(a)), or any extension thereof (37 CFR 41.37(e)), to avoid dismissal of the appeal. Since a Notice of Appeal has been filed, any reply must be filed within the time period set forth in 37 CFR 41.37(a).

AMENDMENTS

3. [ ] The proposed amendment(s) filed after a final rejection, but prior to the date of filing a brief, will not be entered because

(a) [ ] They raise new issues that would require further consideration and/or search (see NOTE below);

(b) [ ] They raise the issue of new matter (see NOTE below):

(c) [ ] They are not deemed to place the application in better form for appeal by materially reducing or simplifying the issues for appeal; and/or

(d} [ ] They present additional claims without canceling a corresponding number of finally rejected claims. NOTE: __. (See 37 CFR 1.116 and 41.33(a)).

4. [X] The amendments are not in compliance with 37 CFR 1.121. See attached Notice of Non·Compliant Amendment (PTOl-324).

5. **[ ]** Applicant's reply has overcome the following rejection(s):__.

6. **[ ]** Newly proposed or amended claim(s}__would be allowable if submitted in a separate, timely filed amendment canceling the

non-allowable claim(s).

7. **[X]** For purposes of appeal, the proposed amendment(s}: a) **[X]** will not be entered, or b) **[ ]** will be entered and an explanation of how the new or amended claims would be rejected is provided below or appended.

The status of the claim(s) is (or will be) as follows:

Claim(s} allowed:__.

Claim(s} objected to: __.

Claim(s} rejected: **<u>1 - 10</u>**.

Claim(s} withdrawn from consideration: __

<u>AFFIDAVIT OR OTHER EVIDENCE</u>

8. **[ ]** The affidavit or other evidence filed after a final action, but before or on the date of filing a Notice of Appeal will <u>not</u> be entered because applicant failed to provide a showing of good and sufficient reasons why the affidavit or other evidence is necessary and was not earlier presented. See 37 CFR 1.116(e).

9. **[ ]** The affidavit or other evidence filed after the date of filing a Notice of Appeal, but prior to the date of filing a brief, will not be entered because the affidavit or other evidence failed to overcome all rejections under appeal and/or appellant fails to provide a showing a good and sufficient reasons why it is necessary and was not earlier presented. See 37 CFR 41.33(d)(1).

10. **[ ]** The affidavit or other evidence is entered. An explanation of the status of the claims after entry is below or attached.

<u>REQUEST FOR RECONSIDERATION/OTHER</u>

11. **[X]** The request for reconsideration has been considered but does NOT place the application in condition for allowance because:

<u>See Continuation Sheet.</u>

12. [ ] Note the attached Information Disc/or use *Statement(s).* (PTO/SB/08) Paper No(s}.__
13. [ ] Other:__.

{Duc NguyenJ
Supervisory Patent Examiner, Art Unit 2618

U.S, Patent and Trademark Office

-- Page 3

Continuation Sheet (PTO-303) Application No. *10/905,635*

Continuation of 11. does NOT place the application in condition for allowance because: The filed amendment is not in compliant and the applicant did not sign properly.

-- Page 4

***Notice* of *Non-Compliant Amendment* (37 *CFR* 1.121**

Application No. *10/905.635* Art Unit 2618
Applicant(s) KOGAN, ILYA
Examiner AJIBOLA AKINYEMI
The *MAIUNG DA TE of this communication appears on the cover sheet with the correspondence address -*

-

The amendment document filed on 12 *September 2008* is considered non-compliant because it has failed to meet the requirements of 37 CFR 1.121 or 1.4. In order for the amendment document to be compliant, correction of the following item(s) is required.

THE FOLLOWING MARKED (**X**) ITEM(S) CAUSE THE AMENDMENT DOCUMENT TO BE NON-COMPLIANT:

[ ] 1. Amendments to the specification:

[ ] A. Amended paragraph(s) do not include markings.

[ ] B. New paragraph(s) should not be underlined.

[[C. Other__.

[ ] 2. Abstract:

[ ] A. Not presented on a separate sheet. 37 CFR 1.72.

[ ] B. Other__.

[ ] 3. Amendments to the drawings:

[ ] A. The drawings are not property identified in the top margin as "Replacement Sheet: "New Sheet," or "Annotated Sheet" as required by 37 CFR 1.121(d).

[ ] B. The practice of submitting proposed drawing correction has been eliminated. Replacement drawings showing amended figures, without markings, in compliance with 37 CFR 1.84 are required.

[ ] C Other--

[ ] 4. Amendments to the claims:

[ ] A. A complete listing of all of the claims is not present.

[ ] B. The listing of claims does not include the text of all pending claims (including withdrawn claims)

[ ] C. Each claim has not been provided with the proper status identifier, and as such, the individual status of each claim cannot be identified. Note: the status of every claim must be indicated after its claim number by using one of the following status identifiers: (Original), (Currently amended), (Canceled),

(Previously presented), (New), (Not entered), (Withdrawn) and (Withdrawn-currently amended).

[ ] D. The claims of this amendment paper have not been presented in ascending numerical order.

[ ] E. Other:__.

[X] 5. Other (e.g., the amendment is unsigned or not signed in accordance with 37 CFR 1.4):

Applicant needs to properly sign the amendment submitted on *09/12f2008.*

For further explanation of the amendment format required by 37 CFR 1.121, see MPEP § 714.

TIME PERIODS FOR FILING A REPLY TO THIS NOTICE:

1 Applicant is given no new time period if the non-compliant amendment is an after-final amendment or an amendment filed after allowance. If applicant wishes to resubmit the non-compliant after-final amendment with corrections, the entire corrected amendment must be resubmitted.

2. Applicant is given one month, or thirty (30) days, whichever is longer, from the mail date of this notice to supply the correction, if the non-compliant amendment is one of the following: a preliminary amendment, a non-final amendment (including a submission for a request for continued examination (RCE) under 37 CFR 1.114), a supplemental amendment filed within a suspension period under 37 CFR 1.103(a) or (c). and an amendment filed in response to a *Quayle* action. If any of above boxes 1. to 4. are checked, the correction required is only the corrected section of the non-compliant amendment in compliance with 37 CFR 1.121.

Extensions of time are available under 37 CFR 1.136(a) only if the non-compliant amendment is a non-final amendment or an amendment filed in response to a *Quayle* action.

Failure to timely respond to this notice will result in: Abandonment of the application if the non-compliant amendment is a non-final amendment or an amendment filed in response to a *Quayle* action; or Non-entry of the amendment if the non-compliant amendment is a preliminary amendment or supplemental amendment.

/Duc Nguyen!
Supervisory Patent Examiner, Art Unit 2618

U.S. Patent and Trademark Office

3.7. Reply to the USPTO Document from 11-24-2008, sent 12-05-2008

To: Commissioner for Patents,
US Patent and Trademark Office
P.O. Box 1450,
Alexandria, VA 22313 - 1450

From: Ilya Kogan
2573 E 27 St., Brooklyn NY 11235,
kogani@optonline.net, 718/769-8637

Re: Office Action Summaries to app. No. 10/905635, art unit 2618 from 08/29/2008, and from 10/22/2007 conf. no. 2635; and Letter
from USPTO art unit 2618 from 11/24.2008

Dear Sir, Madam,

1. On 11/24/2008, it was sent the third answer, "Advisory Action" (about the time for an answer see pos. 3). It seemed that the only problem is a bad signature. **I attach to this letter (only to USPTO) the necessary document** (dated *09/10/2008,* and delivered, according to USPTO stamp on 9/11/2008) **with my signature.**

On *08129/2008,* it was sent the second "Office Action Summary". It was marked as **FINAL REJECTION**, and it was given three month for an answer. My reply was *9/10/2008.*

On 10/22/2007, (in about two years, see pos 4) it was sent the first "Office Action Summary". It was marked as non-final, and it was given three month for an answer. My reply was 11/12/2007.

On 01/13/2005, I made an application for a patent, app. No. 10/905635

2. This document is written to prevent stopping the case for a formal reason. However, I am not sure that this is possible (see pos. 3). I have feeling, that my arguments would be ignored, as it was earlier. It is quite possible, that once more would be repeated the same USPTO fabrications, as if in some, pointed by USPTO applications, my proposals already exist. I want to stress, there is no necessity to prepare reasons against USPTO, and it is obvious, that they have nothing to do with reality. It is easy to show, that my previous answers were ignored. The goal to reject my application is obvious **(this does not prove that my application deserves a patent)**. However, it should not be rejected by far-fetched reasons, which are copied from one "Office Action Summary" into another. This could be done by persons who are completely sure in their permissiveness. Their behavior does not have a smallest degree of logic, common sense, or objectivity. However, their persistence shows a goal only" known by them, which conflicts with my application.

I do not know what for exists the USPTO. In my case, its work is at least strange. In their "Office Action Summary" are written thing that are alleged in some application, which is completely wrong. When I write that in the mentioned application does not exist this, it is simply ignored. They repeated the same text from the first document copying the previous pages word by word and do their conclusion as if the unreal may ever become true. It is necessary to stress, there is not any mention, that my answer in any way is not correct.

The first Office Action Summary rejected all my claims. It was written that in some another application there was the same (it may happen). However, when I read the mentioned application, there was nothing of the kind. There were no words or even meaning, which was written in the USPTO "Office Action Summary" from 10/22/2007. I wrote an answer *(11112/2007)*, in which this was shown. Remarks about the form of the document I corrected and this was accepted by USPTO, because this not mentioned in the next "Office Action Summary".

In about ten months, I received the second Office Action Summary with final rejection for all my claims. When I read it, I find out that it is a copy (an exact copy, a single word was not added!) of the text from the first one. I understand that in such situation it is useless to apply to USPTO for any reasonable discussion. Even so, I sent to USPTO a solid background, which shows that all their remarks have nothing to do with reality. In my answer dated 11/12/2007, I wrote, Analysis of your text and my answers leads to the conclusion, that you have Knoble application text that principally differs from one in Pub. No.: US 2002/0068529Al as it is published by USPTO. The same is

related to other applications mentioned by USPTO. The last phrases I repeated in my answer from *9/1012008.* **On the official USPTO site, one can read the entire necessary document. This allows verifying the correctness of written above.**

3. The marked position in USPTO "Advisory Action" from *11/24/2008* states (Pas. 1.b.), ***"The period for reply expires on:* (1) *the mailing date of this Advisory Action ...*** ". Do not smile; this is very serious! Unbelievable, but at the end of the letter I was given one month for a reply.

4. It is written, that my reply from 9/1 0/2008 was not properly signed and **attach to this letter (only to USPTO) the same document with my signature.** On the other hand, for the years the USPTO does its job, I got essential tremor and my handwriting (and signature) became very bad. In addition, such long period allow to became obsolete any invention, what did unbelievable harm to our country.

I state, that all the content of the both "Office Action Summary" related to rejection of positions in my application

must be thrown out. Instead must be something real. Consequently, I decided to apply for justice.

Sincerely *(signature)* Ilya Kogan

December 5, 2008

ATTACHMENT, (Only to USPTO) Signed answer to Office Action Summary from *08/29/2008* to app. No. 10/905635. This is a copy of my answer mailed on 09/10/2008

3.8. 03-02-2009, USPTO Non-Final Rejection

(This is unexpected non-final rejection after USPTO final rejection from 08-29-2008)

Page

2

Application/Control Number: 10/905,635
Art Unit: 2618

DETAILED ACTION

1. Applicant's request for reconsideration of the finality of the rejection of the last Office action is persuasive and, therefore, the finality of that action is withdrawn.

The following guidelines illustrate the preferred layout for the specification of a utility application. These guidelines are suggested for the applicant's use.

Arrangement of the Specification

As provided in 37 CFR 1.77(b), the specification of a utility application should include the following sections in order. Each of the lettered items should appear in upper case, without underlining or bold type, as a section heading. If no text follows the section heading, the phrase "Not Applicable" should follow the section heading:

(a) TITLE OF THE INVENTION.
(b) CROSS-REFERENCE TO RELATED APPLICATIONS.
(c) STATEMENT REGARDING FEDERALLY SPONSORED RESEARCH OR DEVELOPMENT.

(d) THE NAMES OF THE PARTIES TO A JOINT RESEARCH AGREEMENT.

(e) INCORPORATION-BY-REFERENCE OF MATERIAL SUBMITTED ON A COMPACT DISC.

(f) BACKGROUND OF THE INVENTION.

(1) Field of the Invention.

(2) Description of Related Art including information disclosed under 37

CFR 1.97 and 1.98.

(g) BRIEF SUMMARY OF THE INVENTION.

(h) BRIEF DESCRIPTION OF THE SEVERAL VIEWS OF THE DRAWING(S).

(i) DETAILED DESCRIPTION OF THE INVENTION.

(j) CLAIM OR CLAIMS (commencing on a separate sheet).

(k) ABSTRACT OF THE DISCLOSURE (commencing on a separate sheet).

(l) SEQUENCE LISTING (See MPEP § 2424 and 37 CFR 1.821-1.825. A "Sequence Listing" is required on paper if the application discloses a nucleotide or amino acid sequence as defined in 37 CFR 1.821 (a) and if the required "Sequence Listing" is not submitted as an electronic document on compact disc.

Page 3

Application/Control Number: 10/905,635
Art Unit: 2618

Content of Specification

(a) Title of the Invention: See 37 CFR 1.72(a) and MPEP § 606. The title of the invention should be placed at the top of the first page of the specification unless the title is provided in an application data sheet. The title of the invention should be brief but technically accurate and descriptive, preferably from two to seven words may not contain more than 500 characters.

(b) Cross-References to Related Applications: See 37 CFR 1.78 and MPEP § 201.11.

(c) Statement Regarding Federally Sponsored Research and Development: See MPEP § 310.

(d) The Names Of The Parties To A Joint Research Agreement: See 37 CFR 1.71(g).

(e) Incorporation-By-Reference of Material Submitted on a Compact Disc: The specification is required to include an incorporation-by-reference of electronic documents that are to become part of the permanent United States Patent and Trademark Office records in the file of a patent application. See 37 CFR 1.52(e) and MPEP § 608.05. Computer program listings (37 CFR 1.96(c)), "Sequence Listings" (37 CFR 1.821 (c)), and tables having more than 50 pages of text were permitted as electronic documents on compact discs beginning on September 8,2000.

(f) Background of the Invention: See MPEP § 608.01 (c). The specification should set forth the Background of the Invention in two parts:

(1) Field of the Invention: A statement of the field of art to which the invention pertains. This statement may include a paraphrasing of the applicable U.S. patent classification definitions of the subject matter of the claimed invention. This item may also be titled "Technical Field."

(2) Description of the Related Art including information disclosed under 37 CFR 1.97 and 37 CFR 1.98: A

description of the related art known to the applicant and including, if applicable, references to specific related art and problems involved in the prior art which are solved by the applicant's invention. This item may also be titled "Background Art."

Page 4

Application/Control Number: 10/905,635
Art Unit: 2618

(g) Brief Summary of the Invention: See MPEP § 608.01 (d). A brief summary or general statement of the invention as set forth in 37 CFR 1.73. The summary is separate and distinct from the abstract and is directed toward the invention rather than the disclosure as a whole. The summary may point out the advantages of the invention or how it solves problems previously existent in the prior art (and preferably indicated in the Background of the Invention). In chemical cases, it should point out in general terms the utility of the invention. If possible, the nature and gist of the invention or the inventive concept should be set forth. Objects of the invention should be treated briefly and only to the extent that they contribute to an understanding of the invention.

(h) **Brief Description of the Several Views of the Drawing(s):** See MPEP § 608.01 (f). A reference to and brief description of the drawing(s) as set forth in 37 CFR 1.74.

(i) Detailed Description of the Invention: See MPEP § 608.01 (g). A description of the preferred embodiment(s) of the invention as required in 37 CFR 1.71. The description should be as short and specific as is necessary to describe the invention adequately and accurately. Where elements or groups of elements, compounds, and processes, which are conventional and generally widely known in the field of the invention described and their exact nature or type is not necessary for an understanding and use of the invention by a person skilled in the art, they should not be described in detail. However, where particularly complicated subject matter is involved or where the elements, compounds, or processes may not be commonly or widely known in the field, the specification should refer to another patent or readily available publication, which adequately describes the subject matter.

(j) Claim or Claims: See 37 CFR 1.75 and MPEP § 608.01 (m). The claim or claims must commence on separate sheet or electronic page (37 CFR 1.52(b)(3)). Where a claim sets forth a plurality of elements or steps, each element or step of the claim should be separated by a line indentation. There may be plural indentations to further segregate sub combinations or related steps. See 37 CFR 1.75 and MPEP § 608.01 (i)-(p).

(k) Abstract of the Disclosure: See MPEP § 608.01 (f). A brief narrative of the disclosure as a whole in a single paragraph of 150 words or less commencing on a separate sheet following the claims. In an international application which has entered the national stage (37 CFR 1.491 (b)), the applicant need not submit an abstract commencing on a separate sheet if an abstract was published with the international application under PCT Article 21. The abstract that appears on the cover page of the pamphlet published by the International Bureau (IB) of the World Intellectual

Page 5

Application/Control Number: 10/905,635
Art Unit: 2618

Property Organization (WIPO) is the abstract that will be used by the USPTO. See MPEP § 1893.03(e).

(l) Sequence Listing. See 37 CFR 1.821-1.825 and MPEP §§ 2421-2431. The requirement for a sequence listing applies to all sequences disclosed in a given application, whether the sequences are claimed or not. See MPEP § 2421.02.

1. An examination of this application reveals that applicant is unfamiliar with patent prosecution procedure. While an inventor may prosecute the application, lack of skill in this field usually acts as a liability in affording the maximum protection for the invention disclosed. Applicant is advised to secure the services of a registered patent attorney or agent to prosecute the application, since the value of a patent is largely dependent upon skilled preparation and prosecution. The Office cannot aid in selecting an attorney or agent.

A listing of registered patent attorneys and agents is available on the USPTO Internet web site http://www.uspto.gov in the Site Index under "Attorney and Agent Roster." Applicants may also obtain a list of registered patent attorneys and agents located in their area by writing to the Mail Stop OED, Director of the U. S. Patent and Trademark Office, PO Box 1450, Alexandria, VA 22313-1450. The applicant also can contact the Inventor Assistance Center at 800-PTO-9199 or 571-272-1000 for helps.

***Claim Rejections* - 35 *USC* § 112**

2. The following is a quotation of the first paragraph of 35 U.S.C. 112:

The specification shall contain a written description of the invention, and of the manner and process of making and using it, in such full, clear, concise, and exact terms as to enable any person skilled in the

Page 6

Application/Control Number: 10/905,635
Art Unit: 2618

art to which it pertains, or with which it is most nearly connected, to make and use the same and shall set forth the best mode contemplated by the inventor of carrying out his invention.

3. Claims 1-10 are rejected under 35 U.S.C. 112, first paragraph, as failing to comply with the enablement requirement. The claim(s) contains subject matter, which was not described in the specification in such a way as to enable one skilled in the art to which it pertains, or with which it is most nearly connected, to make and/or use the invention. The structure which goes to make up the device **was not** clearly and positively specified. The structure **was not** organized and correlated in such a way as to enable one skilled in the art to which it pertains, or with which it is most nearly connected, to make and/or use the invention.

1. The following is a quotation of the second paragraph of 35 U.S.C. 112:

The specification shall conclude with one or more claims particularly pointing out and distinctly claiming the subject matter, which the applicant regards as his invention.

2. Claims 1-10 are rejected as failing to define the invention in the manner required by 35 U.S.C. 112, second paragraph.

The claim(s) are narrative in form and replete with indefinite and functional or operational language. **The structure, which goes to make up the device, must be clearly and positively specified. The structure must be organized and correlated in such a manner as to present a complete operative device.** The claim(s) must be in one sentence form only. Note the format of the claims in the patent(s) cited.

Page 7

Application/Control Number: 10/905,635
Art Unit: 2618

4. Regarding claims 2, 7-8 the phrase "e.g.," renders the claim indefinite because it is unclear whether the limitation(s) following the phrase are part of the claimed invention. See MPEP § 2173.05(d).

5. The claims are generally narrative and indefinite, failing to conform to current U.S. practice. They are replete with grammatical and idiomatic errors.

6. Claims 1-10 are rejected under 35 U.S.C. 112, second paragraph, as being indefinite for failing to particularly point out and distinctly claim the subject matter which applicant regards as the invention. Regarding claims 1-2, 10, it is not clear whether the recited elements enclosed within the parentheses are part of the claims or not.

7. Claims 1-10 provide for the use of a cellular phone for a variety of usage purposes, but, since the claims does not set forth any steps involved in the method/process, it is unclear what method/process applicant is intending to encompass. A

claim is indefinite where it merely recites a use without any active, positive steps delimiting how this use is actually practiced.

Claims 1-10 are rejected under 35 U.S.C. 101 because the claimed recitation of a use, without setting forth any steps involved in the process, results in an improper definition of a process, i.e., results in a claim which is not a proper process claim under 35 U.S.C. 101. See for example *Ex Parte Dunki,* 153 USPQ 678 (Bd.App. 1967) and *Clinical Products, Ltd.* v. *Brenner,* 255 F. Supp. 131,149 USPQ 475 (DD.C. 1966).

Page 8

Application/Control Number: 10/905,635
Art Unit: 2618

Claim Rejections* - 35 *USC* § *102

8. The following is a quotation of the appropriate paragraphs of 35 U.S.C. 102 that form the basis for the rejections under this section made in this Office action:

A person shall be entitled to a patent unless –

(b) the invention was patented or described in a printed publication in this or a foreign country, in public use, or on sale in this country, more than one year prior to the date of application for patent in the United States.

9. Claims 1-3, 5-10 are rejected under 35 U.S.C. 102(b) as being anticipated by Meade (Pub. No.: US 2003/0071117A1).

<u>With respect to claim 1</u>:

Meade discloses a method which allows (a) with minor changes in the modem cellular phone and without any additional devices to eliminate and simplify usage of many electronic and communication devices of everyday life **(fig.2, item 12 which is a PDA is being used to control different items 13);** (b) the proposed method enlarges the efficiency of the devices by implementing standard connections; (c) it allows simplifying and making cheaper the usage of the more and more necessary and widely used devices,(d) the method allows (due to the modem multi functional cellular phone) to decrease the number of necessary equipment,(item **12 in fig.2 is being used to control all these items 13 rather than having separate remote control for each)** (e) the method claims also to use a cellular phone as an input to a hub from which are working many home devices **(item 12 in fig. 2 which is PDA is used as a hub for all these items 13).**

Page 9

Application/Control Number: 10/905,635
Art Unit: 2618

With respect to claim 2:

Meade discloses a method, according to claim 1 that allows to eliminate any special connection to the internet such as cable or telephone line **(fig.2, item 12 which is PDA can be connected to a item 36 which is a website without any cable);** the PC has such means and modem cellular phones have to some extent such possibilities as well, but for some reasons they are not standard, but individual for near every phone model (e.g. cables for connection to USB has near every cell phone, but nowadays they are different) **(fig.2, item 12 which is PDA can be connected to a item 36 which is a website without any cable)**

With respect to claim 3:

Meade discloses a method according to claim 1 that allows to receive TV programs and videophone conversations on big TV or PC screens directly through the cellular phone **(parag. 0027),** the cellular phones have such possibilities; today's TV does not;

temporarily can be used a coaxial cable output from the cellular phone, or any other available in TV; in the nearest future all digital TV would have a USB input, a USB output from a cellular phone already exists **(parag. 0027).**

With respect to claim 5:

Meade discloses a method according to claim 1 that allows to use a conventional stationary phone without a phone line and without any additional adapters or other devices; this needs only some minor changes in the cellular phone, comparing to the

Page 10

Application/Control Number: 10/905,635
Art Unit: 2618

functions the cellular phones already have this addition is minor; it is necessary to stress that similar features for other purposes already exist in the cellular phones, temporary, it is necessary to have a cable, which has from one end connection to the cellular phone and from the other end a standard telephone connection; in the future, the stationary phones should have USB input **(Parag. 0090 and 0091).**

With respect to claim 6:

Meade discloses a method according to claim 5 that allows eliminating the necessity of telephone lines and does not bind the telephone position next to the line outlet; the widening of cellular phone usage would make it cheaper **(fig.7, parag. 0090-0091).**

With respect to claim 7:

Meade discloses a method according to claim 1 that allows to use the cellular phone with any standard devices that have a USB input, e.g. printers, to print the pictures directly from the cellular phone; or VCRs **(see fig 2, item 24).**

With respect to claim 8:

Meade discloses a method according to claims 5 that makes it necessary to create stationary phones with some functions of a cellular phone, this follow from the widening usage of cellular phones and necessity of more channels, as now it makes necessity for additional tracks for stationary phone lines, e.g. for internet; in addition, the standard

Page 11

Application/Control Number: 10/905,635
Art Unit: 2618

telephone line does not support some functions of the cellular phones due to frequency limitations (fig.7, parag.0090-0091).

With respect to claim 9:

Meade discloses a method according to claims 8 that allows to use the cellular phone as an input to a slightly modernized, hub for transferring the signals to different devices (fig. 2, item 12 is serving as an input to Hub for various items 13).

With respect to claim 10:

Meade discloses a method according to claim 1 that makes it useful to create stationary phones with (wireless) connection to a hub in addition to the existing connection with multiple wireless handsets **(fig.7).**

Claim Rejections - **35** *USC* **§** *103*

10. The following is a quotation of 35 U.S.C. 103(a) which forms the basis for all obviousness rejections set forth in this Office action:

(a) A patent may not be obtained though the invention is not identically disclosed or described as set forth in section 102 of this title, if the differences between the subject matter sought to be patented and the prior art are such that the subject matter as a whole would have been obvious at the time the invention was made to a person having ordinary skill in the art to which said subject matter pertains. Patentability shall not be negatived by the manner in which the invention was made.

11. The factual inquiries set forth in *Graham* v. *John Deere* Co., 383 U.S. 1, 148 USPQ 459 (1966), that are applied for establishing a background for determining obviousness under 35 U.S.C. 03(a) are summarized as follows:

1. Determining the scope and contents of the prior art.

Page 12

Application/Control Number: 10/905,635
Art Unit: 2618

2. Ascertaining the differences between the prior art and the claims at issue.

3. Resolving the level of ordinary skill in the pertinent art.

4. Considering objective evidence present in the application indicating obviousness or no obviousness.

12. Claim 4 is rejected under 35 U.S.C. 103(a) as being unpatentable over Meade (Pub. No.: US 2003/0071117A1) and further in view of McZeal (Patent No.: US 676322681).

<u>With respect to claim 4</u>:

Meade discloses a method which allows (a) with minor changes in the modem cellular phone and without any additional devices to eliminate and simplify usage of many electronic and communication devices of everyday life **(fig.2, item 12 which is a PDA is being used to control different items 13);** (b) the proposed method enlarges the efficiency of the devices by implementing standard connections; (c) it allows simplifying and making cheaper the usage of the more and more necessary and widely used devices,(d) the method allows (due to the modem multi functional cellular phone) to decrease the number of necessary equipment,(item **12 in fig.2 is being used to control all these items 13 rather than having separate remote control for each)** (e) the method claims also to use a cellular phone as an input to a hub from which are working many home devices **(item 12 in fig. 2 which is PDA is used as a hub for all these items 13).** Meade differs from claim invention in that using a cellular phone as a web cam with PC or laptop is not taught.

McZeal teaches a portable phone with web cam (col.21, lines 1-5). It would have been obvious to one of ordinary skill in the art at the time the invention was made to have used a portable phone with a web cam.

Page 13

Application/Control Number: 10/905,635
Art Unit: 2618

Modifying Meade with McZeal invention will help in saving money and eliminate the use of some electronics equipment on a separate basis.

Response to Arguments

The Examiner has examined this application base on best reasonable interpretation of claims 1-10.

Conclusion

Any inquiry concerning this communication or earlier communications from the examiner should be directed to AJIBOLA AKINYEMI whose telephone number is (571)270-1846. The examiner can normally be reached on Monday- Friday (8.30-5pm) Est.

If attempts to reach the examiner by telephone are unsuccessful, the examiner's supervisor, YUWEN PAN can be reached on (571) 272-7855. The fax phone number for the organization where this application or proceeding is assigned is 571-273-8300.

Page 14

Application/Control Number: 10/905,635
Art Unit: 2618

Information regarding the status of an application may be obtained from the Patent Application Information Retrieval (PAIR) system. Status information for published applications may be obtained from either Private PAIR or Public PAIR. Status information for unpublished applications is available through Private PAIR only. For more information about the PAIR system, see http://pair-direct.uspto.gov. Should you have questions on access to the Private PAIR system, contact the Electronic Business Center (EBC) at 866-217-9197 (toll-free). If you would like assistance from a USPTO Customer Service Representative or access to the automated information system, call 800-786-9199 (IN USA OR CANADA) or 571-272-1000.

AA
/Duc Nguyen/
Supervisory Patent Examiner, Art Unit 2618

3.9. Response to USPTO non-final rejection from 03-02-2009

Page 1

To: Commissioner for Patents,

US Patent and Trademark Office
P.O. Box 1450, Alexandria, VA 22313 - 1450

From: Ilya Kogan
2573 E 27 St., Brooklyn NY 11235,
kogani@optonline.net, 718-769-8637

Re: USPTO Office Action Summaries from 03/02/2009 to app. No. 10/905635, art unit 2618

March 30, 2009

Dear Sir or Madam,

After a final rejection of my application by your office due to some obviously far-fetched reasons, I unexpectedly received a new letter that contained not a final rejection. Here, as in the previous two letters from your office, all claims of my application are rejected. However, it is impossible to agree with both the form and the content of the USPTO Office Action Summaries from 03/02/2009.

This document has 14 pages. The pages until p. 5 contain a copy of the rules for preparing applications. Then, partially repeating the rules, all the claims (1 - 10) of my application No.

10/905635 is rejected several times, due to the formal requirements.

After this, on pages 8 – 12 and in one short phrase on page 13, all the claims are rejected once more. This time it is stated that all my claims exist in some other application.

I agree that the form is important; however, it is meaningless to argue this question, if the application is not innovative. Only after the issue of originality is resolved, it would be necessary to correct the form, which of course is possible. That is why below, in Part 1 of my answer, I give the analysis of pages 8 - 12 of the USPTO document, and after that in Part 2, I give an answer to formal rejections and remarks.
All quotations are given in *italic.*

PART 1. ANSWER TO THE PAGES 8 – 12

The USPTO Actions (page 8) says: *9. Claims 1-3, 5-10 are rejected under 35 U.S.C. 102(b) as being anticipated by Meade (Pub. No.: US 2003/0071117A1).*

In all the 14 claims, Meade did not mention any of the following words: phone, cell phone, input line, hub, or PDA. The goal of his invention is to control many appliances by mobile computing devices according to certain algorithms. In the figures that accompany Meade's application, he mentioned various appliances, such as table lamp, coffee maker, cell phone, TV set and many more. **It is clear that my and Meade's applications have completely different goals and from the point of view of their priority and the concept of the invention they do not interfere with each other. These are two different subjects.**

Page 2

Pages 8 – 12 in USPTO Summaries contain about 60 lines. About 50 of them reproduce my claims 1 - 3 and 5 - 10 (instead of copying claim 4, the claim 1 was copied again). In front of every copy of my claim, the reviewer placed the words *Meade discloses.* Inside the copy of each of my claims, the reviewer inserted in brackets, in bold, the brief reasons for rejection. For claims 1, 2, 4, and 9, the reviewer inserted nine times the words ***"(item 12 in fig. 2 which is PDA is used as a hub for all these items 13)"***, or part of it. Once for every claim 5, 6, and 8 was inserted ***(fig.7, parag. 0090-0091)***. For claim 3 was inserted ***(parag. 0027)***. For claim 7 was inserted ***(see fig 2, item 24)***. For claim 10 was inserted **(fig.7)**. This text in bold (it contains about two lines, which are many times repeated) is the complete reason to reject all the claims 1 – 10. For rejecting claim 4, the reviewer copied my claim 1 with the same rejection reasons as for claim 1. Claim 4 was not copied and its content is not mentioned.

1. For claim 1 (page 8), the reasons for rejection by reviewer were:

<u>With respect to claim 1.</u> Meade discloses a method which allows (a) with minor changes in the modem cellular phone and without any additional devices to eliminate and simplify usage of many electronic and communication devices of everyday life ***(fig.2, item 12 which is a PDA is being used to control different items 13);*** *(b) the proposed method enlarges the efficiency of the devices by implementing standard connections; (c) it allows simplifying and making cheaper the usage of the more and more necessary and widely used devices,(d) the method allows (due to the modem multi functional cellular phone) to decrease the number of necessary equipment,* ***(item 12 in fig.2 is being used to control all these items 13 rather than having separate remote control for each)*** *(e) the method claims also to use a cellular phone as an input to a hub from which are working many home devices* ***(item 12 in fig. 2 which is PDA is used as a hub for all these items 13).***

The above quotation is an exact copy of my claim 1 with the words "*Meade discloses*" added in the beginning, with critical remarks given in bold. The reviewer, without any explanation, interprets Meade's figure 2 so that it becomes possible by a short remark, repeated three times, to reject the claim 1.

In the application Pub. No.: US 2003/0071117A1, Meade proposed to control all the appliances of a household (from TV to lamps and refrigerators) with the help of a portable computing device. The reviewer confused and misinterpreted the situation. What I propose is not a change of control devices, which by the way requires principal changes in the existing devices and in standards. I propose to use the cell phone as a main source of input signals instead of many existing and different input lines. This proposal requires only some relatively simple changes in the phone scheme. However, it gives great convenience and advantages. A number of commonly used devices might become not needed. The goal of complete automation and central control for the entire household in my application is not even mentioned. On the other hand, the goal of elimination of input lines is not mentioned by Meade.

Page 3

This shows that the reviewer, accidentally or intentionally, did not understand the principal differences between my and Meade's applications.

The same should be repeated for claims 2, 4, 7, and 9.

2. For claims 5, 6, 8 and 10, reviewer repeated my claims and added *Meade discloses*, e.g. *With respect to claim 6: Meade discloses a method according to claim 5 that allows eliminating the necessity of telephone lines and does not bind the telephone position* *next to the line outlet; the widening of cellular phone usage would make it cheaper* ***(fig.7, parag. 0090-0091).***

Meade wrote commenting on his fig. 7: *[0016] FIG. 7 is a block diagram of a mobile phone, a land-line phone, and a mobile computing device of an appliance control system, according to one embodiment of the present invention.* In the parag. 0090-0091 Meade did not mention input lines of land-line phone. In these paragraphs, as well as in the rest of his application, there is nothing said about eliminating those lines, the primary goal of my application. Meade treats both types of phones as equivalent devices.

3. For claim 3, <u>*With respect to claim 3:*</u>*Meade discloses a method according to claim 1 that allows to receive TV programs and videophone conversations on big TV or PC screens directly through the cellular phone* **(parag. 0027)**, *the cellular phones have such possibilities; today's TV does not; temporarily can be used a coaxial cable output from the cellular phone, or any other available in TV; in the nearest future all digital TV would have a USB input, a USB output from a cellular phone already exists* **(parag. 0027).**

However, Meade's parag. 0027 mentioned a different goal:

[0027] For example, upon entry within a room, the mobile computing device can automatically perform these steps: identify an appliance like a TV; activate the TV; turn the TV to a channel carrying a favorite program; and select a preferred volume level. In the event that the favorite program is not being broadcast, the mobile computing device can supply its own content. In particular, the mobile computing device can retrieve an episode of that program or substitute a program from memory of the mobile computing device, transfer that stored program to the TV, and then command the appliance to play the program.

From the explanations given above it is obvious that the rejection of claims 1 - 10 based on the Pub. No.: US 2003/0071117A1 is incorrect.

PART 2. ANSWER TO THE REMARKS RELATED MOSTLY TO THE FORM OF MY APPLICATION

It is necessary to mention that multiple rejections of all the claims due to the necessity of correction the document form is unjust. It would be enough to make a warning that the application may be rejected if it would not be corrected as required.

Page 4

However, if the application is not original as it stated on the pages 8 - 12, the corrections are useless. All the content of pages in USPTO Summaries preceding page 8 is expressed in the following:

1. An examination of this application reveals that applicant is unfamiliar with patent prosecution procedure. While an inventor may prosecute the application, lack of skill in this field usually acts as a liability in affording the maximum protection for the invention disclosed. Applicant is advised to secure the services of a registered patent attorney or agent to prosecute the application, since the value of a patent is largely dependent upon skilled preparation and prosecution. The Office cannot aid in selecting an attorney or agent.

A listing of registered patent attorneys …

Remarks on the first pages may be divided into two groups. The first one is related to the form of the document. For this, a lawyer is not needed. The rules are clear and could be easily followed. The second requires clear and precise expression for specific ideas. Here a lawyer could even be harmful. I tried to get help from lawyers - specialists in patent applications and ran into some difficulties such as wordy and vague expressions, which may be easily rejected. However, the most serious problem was the misrepresentation of the idea. When I pointed to such issues, the lawyer agreed and told that to escape this we must work together. This would take much more time and money. On the other hand, I did not receive any comments about the application form. Analysis of USPTO publications, including all four publications mentioned in my case shows that they must be rejected under the same rules. **This allows to state that USPTO uses these rules very selectively.**

The very first phrases of my text show that English is not my mother tongue. However, I worked in the USA for 12 years and participated in thousands of long discussions about various systems under design. The participants were high-qualified engineers, financiers, and scientists. There was no single case of misunderstanding of my position. In Russia, where I received all my education and worked for 45 years, the opponents of my publications (above 100), inventions and dissertations were more zealous; however, I could show the injustice of their position.

After a careful analysis of three USPTO statements, it is possible to state that I never met such a categorical position in saying something that does not exist. Something like this I heard (but have never seen signed!) from Soviet party bosses. However, they never reached such absurdity.

In my previous two answers to USPTO two rejections, I demonstrated that none of reviewer's allegations were found in **Pub. No.: US 2002/0068529A1, Pub. No.: US 2005/0070327A1,** and **Patent No.: US 6763226B1.** The last reviewer uses **Pub. No.: US 2003/0071117A1**, where the same patent is mentioned as well, e.g. on page 13 is a phrase: *Modifying Meade with McZeal* (**Patent No.: US 6763226B1)** *invention will help in saving money and eliminate the use of some electronics equipment on a separate basis.*

Page 5

It is wrong to reject something because it could be performed by combining with modification of something that already exists. E.g., the patent for placing the airplane engines under the wings used existing planes with the same engines. For sure, it did not describe the thermodynamics of the engines. The applications used by reviewers have no description of many devices (some of them are completely new and problematic). However, reviewer states that in my application well-known existing devices are mentioned but not described.

It almost seems that USPTO keeps on file certain applications, which could be used to repel others to further apply with the similar claims. Suppose that some application paraphrased an idea from a science fiction. E.g., an idea about complete automation of a house. The reviewer accepts that it is possible with a small pocket computer to control dozens if not hundreds of devices. The fiction writer can give the pocket computer possibility to read thoughts. Has the reviewer seen the control devices of TV, air conditioner, cell phone; the number of their buttons? Does he understand the difference between HUB with 4 and 104 input-exits? The reviewer includes such words (better, notions) as PDA or HUB, which are not even present in the quoted documents. To say nothing about the fact that my application has a completely different goal.

USPTO created (an expensive) system, which allows to copy the text of applications. To see the figures USPTO recommends buying some special software. To copy a phrase from their review (not a page as a picture) one must buy and learn more expensive software system. The applicant is sent to the lawyers. **This reminds of how some lawyers behave with the victims of auto accidents.** Clients are sent to a certain doctor. If the client does not want to have so many procedures from that doctor, there is a big probability that the lawyer would not continue the case.

USPTO does not work free; however, the work with an application takes many years. As the result, the implementation of new technologies is deferred for many years. The technologies may become obsolete and the USA lags behind other countries. **The economic and moral damage is tremendous. This influences the USA authority, enlarges the negative trade balance, increases unemployment, and much more.**

Could the reader believe the facts in my answers? It looks impossible, but it is true. All the three USPTO conclusions do not reject anything in my application. **That is why I could not add anything that defends my application or proofs that it deserves a patent,** because to refute anything not connected to the matter under discussion adds nothing. **However, it is impossible to agree with the USPTO Office Action Summaries from 03/02/2009 to app. No. 10/905635, art unit 2618.**

Sincerely Ilya Kogan

3.10. 05-17-2010 USPTO Final Rejection

(The Second final rejection.)

Page 2

Application/Control Number: 10/905,635
Art Unit: 2618

DETAILED ACTION

1. Applicant's request for reconsideration of the finality of the rejection of the last Office action is persuasive and, therefore, the finality of that action is withdrawn.

The following guidelines illustrate the preferred layout for the specification of a utility application. These guidelines are suggested for the applicant's use.

Arrangement of the Specification

As provided in 37 CFR 1.77(b), the specification of a utility application should include the following sections in order. Each of the lettered items should appear in upper case, without underlining or bold type, as a section heading. If no text follows the section heading, the phrase "Not Applicable" should follow the section heading:

(a) TITLE OF THE INVENTION.
(b) CROSS-REFERENCE TO RELATED APPLICATIONS.
(c) STATEMENT REGARDING FEDERALLY SPONSORED RESEARCH OR DEVELOPMENT.
(d) THE NAMES OF THE PARTIES TO A JOINT RESEARCH AGREEMENT.

(e) INCORPORATION-BY-REFERENCE OF MATERIAL SUBMITTED ON A COMPACT DISC.

(f) BACKGROUND OF THE INVENTION.

(1) Field of the Invention.

(2) Description of Related Art including information disclosed under 37 CFR 1.97 and 1.98.

(g) BRIEF SUMMARY OF THE INVENTION.

(h) BRIEF DESCRIPTION OF THE SEVERAL VIEWS OF THE DRAWING(S).

(i) DETAILED DESCRIPTION OF THE INVENTION.

(j) CLAIM OR CLAIMS (commencing on a separate sheet).

(k) ABSTRACT OF THE DISCLOSURE (commencing on a separate sheet).

(l) SEQUENCE LISTING (See MPEP § 2424 and 37 CFR 1.821-1.825. A "Sequence Listing" is required on paper if the application discloses a nucleotide or amino acid sequence as defined in 37 CFR 1.821 (a) and if the required "Sequence Listing" is not submitted as an electronic document on compact disc.

Page 3

Application/Control Number: 10/905,635
Art Unit: 2618

Content of Specification

(a) Title of the Invention: See 37 CFR 1.72(a) and MPEP § 606. The title of the invention should be placed at the top of the first page of the specification unless the title is provided in an application data sheet. The title of the invention should be brief but technically accurate and descriptive, preferably from two to seven words may not contain more than 500 characters.

(b) Cross-References to Related Applications: See 37 CFR 1.78 and MPEP § 201.11.

(c) Statement Regarding Federally Sponsored Research and Development: See MPEP § 310.

(d) The Names Of The Parties To A Joint Research Agreement: See 37 CFR 1.71(g).

(e) Incorporation-By-Reference of Material Submitted on a Compact Disc: The specification is required to include an incorporation-by-reference of electronic documents that are to become part of the permanent United States Patent and Trademark Office records in the file of a patent application. See 37 CFR 1.52(e) and MPEP § 608.05. Computer program listings (37 CFR 1.96(c)), "Sequence Listings" (37 CFR 1.821 (c)), and tables having more than 50 pages of text were permitted as electronic documents on compact discs beginning on September 8, 2000.

(f) Background of the Invention: See MPEP § 608.01 (c). The specification should set forth the Background of the Invention in two parts:

(1) Field of the Invention: A statement of the field of art to which the invention pertains. This statement may include a paraphrasing of the applicable U.S. patent classification definitions of the subject matter of the claimed invention. This item may also be titled "Technical Field."

(2) Description of the Related Art including information disclosed under 37 CFR 1.97 and 37 CFR 1.98: A description of the related art known to the applicant and including, if applicable, references to specific related art and problems involved in the prior art which are solved by the applicant's invention. This item may also be titled "Background Art."

Page 4

Application/Control Number: 10/905,635
Art Unit: 2618

(g) Brief Summary of the Invention: See MPEP § 608.01 (d). A brief summary or general statement of the invention as set forth in 37 CFR 1.73. The summary is separate and distinct from the abstract and is directed toward the invention rather than the disclosure as a whole. The summary may point out the advantages of the invention or how it solves problems previously existent in the prior art (and preferably indicated in the Background of the Invention). In chemical cases, it should point out in general terms the utility of the invention. If possible, the nature and gist of the invention or the inventive concept should be set forth. Objects of the invention should be treated briefly and only to the extent that they contribute to an understanding of the invention.

(h) Brief Description of the Several Views of the Drawing(s): See MPEP § 608.01 (f). A reference to and brief description of the drawing(s) as set forth in 37 CFR 1.74.

(i) Detailed Description of the Invention: See MPEP § 608.01 (g). A description of the preferred embodiment(s) of the invention as required in 37 CFR 1.71. The description should be as short and specific as is necessary to describe the invention adequately and accurately. Where elements or groups of elements, compounds, and processes, which are conventional and generally widely known in the field of the invention described and their exact nature or type is not necessary for an understanding and use of the invention by a person skilled in the art, they should not be described in detail. However, where particularly complicated subject matter is involved or where the elements, compounds, or processes may not be commonly or widely known in the field, the specification should refer to another patent or readily available publication, which adequately describes the subject matter.

j) Claim or Claims: See 37 CFR 1.75 and MPEP § 608.01 (m). The claim or claims must commence on separate sheet or electronic page (37 CFR 1.52(b)(3)). Where a claim sets forth a plurality of elements or steps, each element or step of the claim should be separated by a line indentation. There may be plural indentations to further segregate sub combinations or related steps. See 37 CFR 1.75 and MPEP § 608.01 (i)-(p).

(k) Abstract of the Disclosure: See MPEP § 608.01 (f). A brief narrative of the disclosure as a whole in a single paragraph of 150 words or less commencing on a separate sheet following the claims. In an international application which has entered the national stage (37 CFR 1.491 (b)), the applicant need not submit an abstract commencing on a separate sheet if an abstract was published with the international application under PCT Article 21. The abstract that appears on the cover page of the pamphlet

published by the International Bureau (IB) of the World Intellectual

Page 5

Application/Control Number: 10/905,635
Art Unit: 2618

Property Organization (WIPO) is the abstract that will be used by the USPTO. See MPEP § 1893.03(e).

(l) Sequence Listing. See 37 CFR 1.821-1.825 and MPEP §§ 2421-2431. The requirement for a sequence listing applies to all sequences disclosed in a given application, whether the sequences are claimed or not. See MPEP § 2421.02.

1. An examination of this application reveals that applicant is unfamiliar with patent prosecution procedure. While an inventor may prosecute the application, lack of skill in this field usually acts as a liability in affording the maximum protection for the invention disclosed. Applicant is advised to secure the services of a registered patent attorney or agent to prosecute the application, since the value of a patent is largely dependent upon skilled preparation and prosecution. The Office cannot aid in selecting an attorney or agent.

A listing of registered patent attorneys and agents is available on the USPTO Internet web site ttp://www.uspto.gov in the Site Index under "Attorney and Agent Roster." Applicants may also obtain a list of registered patent attorneys and agents located in their area by writing to the Mail Stop OED, Director of the U. S. Patent and Trademark Office, PO Box 1450, Alexandria, VA 22313-1450

The applicant also can contact the Inventor Assistance Center at 800-PTO-9199 or 571-272-1000 for helps.

***Claim Rejections* - 35 *USC* § 112**

2. The following is a quotation of the first paragraph of 35 U.S.C. 112:

The specification shall contain a written description of the invention, and of the manner and process of making and using it, in such full, clear, concise, and exact terms as to enable any person skilled in the

Page 6

Application/Control Number: 10/905,635
Art Unit: 2618

art to which it pertains, or with which it is most nearly connected, to make and use the same and shall set forth the best mode contemplated by the inventor of carrying out his invention.

3. Claims 1-10 are rejected under 35 U.S.C. 112, first paragraph, as failing to comply with the enablement requirement. The claim(s) contains subject matter, which was not described in the specification in such a way as to enable one skilled in the art to which it pertains, or with which it is most nearly connected, to make and/or use the invention. The structure, which goes to make up the device, **was not** clearly and positively specified. The structure **was not** organized and correlated in such a way as to enable one skilled in the art to which it pertains, or with which it is most nearly connected, to make and/or use the invention.

1. The following is a quotation of the second paragraph of 35 U.S.C. 112:

The specification shall conclude with one or more claims particularly pointing out and distinctly claiming the subject matter, which the applicant regards as his invention.

2. Claims 1-10 are rejected as failing to define the invention in the manner required by 35 U.S.C. 112, second paragraph. The claim(s) are narrative in form and replete with indefinite and functional or operational language. **The structure,**

which goes to make up the device, must be clearly and positively specified. The structure must be organized and correlated in such a manner as to present a complete operative device. The claim(s) must be in one sentence form only. Note the format of the claims in the patent(s) cited.

Page 7

Application/Control Number: 10/905,635
Art Unit: 2618

4. Regarding claims 2, 7-8 the phrase "e.g.," renders the claim indefinite because it is unclear whether the limitation(s) following the phrase are part of the claimed invention. See MPEP § 173.05(d).

5. The claims are generally narrative and indefinite, failing to conform with current U.S. practice. They are replete with grammatical and idiomatic errors.

6. Claims 1-10 are rejected under 35 U.S.C. 112, second paragraph, as being indefinite for failing to particularly point out and distinctly claim the subject matter which applicant regards as the invention.

Regarding claims 1-2, 10, it is not clear whether the recited elements enclosed within the parentheses are part of the claims or not.

7. Claims 1-10 provide for the use of a cellular phone for a variety of usage purposes, but, since the claims does not set forth any steps involved in the method/process, it is unclear what method/process applicant is intending to encompass. A claim is indefinite where it merely recites a use without any active, positive steps delimiting how this use is actually practiced.

Claims 1-10 are rejected under 35 U.S.C. 101 because the claimed recitation of a use, without setting forth any steps involved in the process, results in an improper definition of a process, i.e., results in a claim which is not a proper process claim under 35 U.S.C. 101. See for example *Ex Parte Dunki,* 153 USPQ 678 (Bd.App. 1967) and *Clinical Products, Ltd.* v. *Brenner,* 255 F. Supp. 131,149 USPQ 475 (DD.C. 1966).

Page 8

Application/Control Number: 10/905,635
Art Unit: 2618

Claim Rejections - 35 USC § 102

8. The following is a quotation of the appropriate paragraphs of 35 U.S.C. 102 that form the basis for the rejections under this section made in this Office action:

A person shall be entitled to a patent unless -
(b) the invention was patented or described in a printed publication in this or a foreign country, in public use, or on sale in this country, more than one year prior to the date of application for patent in the United States.

9. Claims 1-3, 5-10 are rejected under 35 U.S.C. 102(b) as being anticipated by Meade (Pub. No.: US 2003/0071117A1).

<u>With respect to claim 1</u>:

Meade discloses a method which allows (a) with minor changes in the modem cellular phone and without any additional devices to eliminate and simplify usage of many electronic and communication devices of everyday life **(fig.2, item 12 which is a PDA is being used to control different items 13);** (b) the proposed method enlarges the efficiency of the devices by implementing standard connections; (c) it allows simplifying and making cheaper the usage of the more and more necessary and widely used devices,(d) the method allows (due to the modem multi functional cellular phone) to decrease the number of necessary equipment,(item **12 in fig.2 is being used to control all these items 13 rather than having separate remote control for each)** (e) the method claims also to use a cellular phone as an input to a hub from which are working many home devices **(item 12 in fig. 2 which is PDA is used as a hub for all these items 13).**

Page 9

Application/Control Number: 10/905,635
Art Unit: 2618

With respect to claim 2:

Meade discloses a method, according to claim 1 that allows to eliminate any special connection to the internet such as cable or telephone line **(fig.2, item 12 which is PDA can be connected to a item 36 which is a website without any cable);** the PC has

such means and modem cellular phones have to some extent such possibilities as well, but for some reasons they are not standard, but individual for near every phone model (e.g. cables for connection to USB has near every cell phone, but nowadays they are different) **(fig.2, item 12 which is PDA can be connected to a item 36 which is a website without any cable)**

With respect to claim 3:

Meade discloses a method according to claim 1 that allows to receive TV programs and videophone conversations on big TV or PC screens directly through the cellular phone **(parag. 0027),** the cellular phones have such possibilities; today's TV does not;

temporarily can be used a coaxial cable output from the cellular phone, or any other available in TV; in the nearest future all digital TV would have a USB input, a USB output from a cellular phone already exists **(parag. 0027).**

With respect to claim 5:

Meade discloses a method according to claim 1 that allows to use a conventional stationary phone without a phone line and without any additional adapters or other devices; this needs only some minor changes in the cellular phone, comparing to the

Page 10

Application/Control Number: 10/905,635
Art Unit: 2618

functions the cellular phones already have this addition is minor; it is necessary to stress that similar features for other purposes already exist in the cellular phones, temporary, it is necessary to have a cable, which has from one end connection to the cellular phone and from the other end a standard telephone connection; in the future, the stationary phones should have USB input **(Parag. 0090 and 0091).**

With respect to claim 6:

Meade discloses a method according to claim 5 that allows eliminating the necessity of telephone lines and does not bind the telephone position next to the line outlet; the widening of cellular phone usage would make it cheaper **(fig.7, parag. 0090-0091).**

With respect to claim 7:

Meade discloses a method according to claim 1 that allows to use the cellular phone with any standard devices that have a USB input, e.g. printers, to print the pictures directly from the cellular phone; or VCRs **(see fig 2, item 24).**

With respect to claim 8:

Meade discloses a method according to claims 5 that makes it necessary to create stationary phones with some functions of a cellular phone, this follow from the widening usage of cellular phones and necessity of more channels, as now it makes necessity for additional tracks for stationary phone lines, e.g. for internet; in addition, the standard

Page 11

Application/Control Number: 10/905,635
Art Unit: 2618

telephone line does not support some functions of the cellular phones due to frequency limitations **(fig.7, parag.0090-0091).**

With respect to claim 9:

Meade discloses a method according to claims 8 that allows to use the cellular phone as an input to a slightly modernized, hub for transferring the signals to different devices **(fig. 2, item 12 is serving as an input to Hub for various items 13).**

With respect to claim 10:

Meade discloses a method according to claim 1 that makes it useful to create stationary phones with (wireless) connection to a hub in addition to the existing connection with multiple wireless handsets **(fig.7).**

Claim Rejections - 35 USC § 103

10. The following is a quotation of 35 U.S.C. 103(a) which forms the basis for all obviousness rejections set forth in this Office action:

(a) A patent may not be obtained though the invention is not identically disclosed or described as set forth in section 102 of this title, if the differences between the subject matter sought to be patented and the prior art are such that the subject matter as a whole would have been obvious at the time the invention was made to a person having ordinary skill in the art to which said subject matter pertains. Patentability shall not be negatived by the manner in which the invention was made.

11. The factual inquiries set forth in *Graham* v. *John Deere* Co., 383 U.S. 1, 148 USPQ 459 (1966), that are applied for establishing a background for determining obviousness under 35 U.S.C. 03(a) are summarized as follows:

1. Determining the scope and contents of the prior art.

Page 12

Application/Control Number: 10/905,635
Art Unit: 2618

2. Ascertaining the differences between the prior art and the claims at issue.
3. Resolving the level of ordinary skill in the pertinent art.
4. Considering objective evidence present in the application indicating obviousness or no obviousness.

12. Claim 4 is rejected under 35 U.S.C. 103(a) as being unpatentable over Meade (Pub. No.: US 2003/0071117A1) and further in view of McZeal (Patent No.: US 676322681).

With respect to claim 4:

Meade discloses a method which allows (a) with minor changes in the modem cellular phone and without any additional devices to eliminate and simplify usage of many electronic and communication devices of everyday life **(fig.2, item 12 which is a PDA is being used to control different items 13);** (b) the proposed method enlarges the efficiency of the devices by implementing standard connections; (c) it allows simplifying and making cheaper the usage of the more and more necessary and widely used devices,(d) the method allows (due to the modem multi functional cellular phone) to decrease the number of necessary equipment,(item **12 in fig.2 is being used to control all these items 13 rather than having separate remote control for each)** (e) the method claims also to use a cellular phone as an input to a hub from which are working many home devices **(item 12 in fig. 2 which is PDA is used as a hub for all these items 13).** Meade differs from claim invention in that using a cellular phone as a web cam with PC or laptop is not taught. McZeal teaches a portable phone with web cam (coI.21, lines 1-5). It would have been obvious to one of ordinary skill in the art at the time the invention was made to have used a portable phone with a web cam.

Page 13
Application/Control Number: 10/905,635
Art Unit: 2618

Modifying Meade with McZeal invention will help in saving money and eliminate the use of some electronics equipment on a separate basis.

Response to Arguments

The Examiner has examined this application base on best reasonable interpretation of claims 1-10.

Conclusion

Any inquiry concerning this communication or earlier communications from the examiner should be directed to AJIBOLA AKINYEMI whose telephone number is (571)270-1846. The examiner can normally be reached on Monday- Friday (8.30-5pm) Est.

If attempts to reach the examiner by telephone are unsuccessful, the examiner's supervisor, YUWEN PAN can be reached on (571) 272-7855. The fax phone number for the organization where this application or proceeding is assigned is 571-273-8300.

Page 14

Application/Control Number: 10/905,635
Art Unit: 2618

Information regarding the status of an application may be obtained from the Patent Application Information Retrieval (PAIR) system. Status information for published applications may be obtained from either Private PAIR or Public PAIR. Status information for unpublished applications is available through Private PAIR only. For more information about the PAIR system, see http://pair-direct.uspto.gov. Should you have questions on access to the Private PAIR system, contact the Electronic Business Center (EBC) at 866-217-9197 (toll-free). If you would like assistance from a USPTO Customer Service Representative or access to the automated information system, call 800-786-9199 (IN USA OR CANADA) or 571-272-1000.

AA
/Duc Nguyen/
Supervisory Patent Examiner, Art Unit 2618

3.11. My response to USPTO document from 5/17/2010
sent 6/2/2010

Page 1

To: Commissioner for Patents,

US Patent and Trademark Office
P.O. Box 1450, Alexandria, VA 22313 - 1450

From: Ilya Kogan
2573 E 27 St., Brooklyn NY 11235,
kogani@optonline.net, 718-769-8637

Re: USPTO Office Action Summaries from 05/17/2010 to app. No. 10/905635, art unit 2618

June 2, 2010

Dear Sir or Madam,

More than five years is enough to understand the entire senselessness of a meaningful discussion with the USPTO. This organization ignores any objections. It does not disprove, it ignores. The same answer without explanations or commentaries is copied from one review into the next one. This permissiveness is unthinkable, not admitted, and must be ceased. Below is proposed the creation of a commission that would contribute to this purpose. Proposals for the creation of this commission would be sent to the Congress of the USA, the Attorney General, and the Inspector General of the US Department of Commerce. Materials also would be sent to most authoritative mass media. In addition to this document was created a site where the documents related to the matter are placed:

http://speculations.us/InIndex/Notebook/History_and_Remarks.htm

PART 1. ANSWER TO THE USPTO AFFIRMATIONS ABOUT THE PRESENCE OF EQUIVALENT CLAIMS IN OTHER APPLICATIONS

The USPTO Office Action Summaries from 05/17/2010 to app. No. 10/905635 contains a final rejection for all claims of my application due to some obviously far-fetched reasons. It is impossible to agree with both the form and the content of the USPTO Office Action Summaries from 05/17/2010.

The USPTO document has 15 pages. The pages, until the middle of page 7, contain a copy of the USPTO rules for preparing applications. Then, partially repeating the rules, all the claims (1 - 10) of my application No. 10/905635 is rejected, due to the formal requirements. Page 12 should be added to this part. The result (on page 5), ***"The office cannot aid in selecting an attorney or agent. A listing of registered ..."*** In this particular case, this advice is completely wrong for the following reasons. On pages 7 - 11 all the claims are rejected once more. This time it is stated, that all my claims exist in some other application. If this is true, what is the reason for editing with an attorney? **I agree that the form is important; however, it is meaningless to argue this question, if the application is not innovative.** That is why I did the analysis of pages 7 -11 and an additional (new) paragraph of the USPTO document on page 13. This paragraph is not copied from the previous USPTO answers. After that in Part 2, I analyze formal remarks.

Page 2

This part of the USPTO summary is an exact copy of previously sent summaries. That is why my answer is near the same as e.g. the one done in 2008. **It is important to mention,**

that one of my answers to the USPTO (with the same text) surprisingly changed the rejection from *final* to *non-final*. All quotations are given in *italic*.

1.1. ANSWER TO THE PAGES 7 - 11

The USPTO Actions (page 7) says, *"9. Claims 1-3, 5-10 are rejected under 35 U.S.C. 102(b) as being anticipated by Meade (Pub. No.: US 2003/0071117A1)"*.

In all the 14 claims, Meade did not mention any of the following words: phone, cell phone, input line, hub, or PDA. The goal of his invention is to control many appliances by mobile computing devices according to certain algorithms. In the figures that accompany Meade's application, he mentioned various appliances, such as a table lamp, coffee maker, cell phone, TV set and many more. **It is clear that my and Meade's applications have completely different goals and from the point of view of their priority and the concept of the invention they do not interfere with each other. These are two different subjects.**

Pages 7 - 11 in USPTO Summaries reproduce my claims 1 - 3 and 5 - 10 (instead of copying claim 4, the claim 1 was copied once more). In front of every copy of my claim, the reviewer placed the words ***"Meade discloses"*. Does this mean that I copied my claim from Meade application? There is nothing of the kind.** Inside the copy of each of my claims, the reviewer inserted in brackets, in bold, the brief reasons for rejection. For claims 1, 2, 4, and 9, the reviewer inserted nine times the words *"**(item 12 in fig. 2 which is PDA is used as a hub for all these items 13)**"*, or part of it. Once for every claim 5, 6, and 8 was inserted *"**(fig.7, parag. 0090-0091)**"*. For claim 3 was inserted *"**(parag. 0027)**"*. For claim 7 was inserted *"**(see fig 2, item 24)**"*. For claim 10 was inserted ***"(fig.7)"*. This text in bold (it contains about two lines, which are many times repeated) is the complete reason to reject all the claims 1 - 10.** For rejecting claim 4, the reviewer copied my claim 1 with the same rejection reasons as for claim 1. Claim 4 was not copied and its content is not mentioned. To prove the above, below are some copies in italic from USPTO Summaries. **I need to repeat, that except for the words "*Meade discloses*" and bold italic text, all the italic text is copied by examiner from my application. It was copied not from Meade application.**

1. For claim 1 (page 7), the reasons for rejection by reviewer were "*With respect to claim 1. Meade discloses a method which allows (a) with minor changes in the modem cellular phone and without any additional devices to eliminate and simplify usage of many electronic and communication devices of everyday life* ***(fig.2, item 12 which is a PDA is being used to control different items 13);*** *(b) the proposed method enlarges the efficiency of the devices by implementing standard connections; (c) it allows simplifying and making cheaper the usage of the more and more necessary and widely used devices,(d) the method allows (due to the modem multi functional cellular phone) to decrease the number of necessary equipment,****(item 12 in fig.2 is being used to control all these items 13 rather than having separate remote control for each)*** *(e) the method*

Page 3

claims also to use a cellular phone as an input to a hub from which are working many home devices ***(item 12 in fig. 2 which is PDA is used as a hub for all these items 13)"***.

The above quotation is an exact copy of my claim 1 with the words "*Meade discloses*" added in the beginning, with critical remarks given in bold. The reviewer, without any explanation, interprets Meade's figure 2 so that it becomes possible by a short remark, repeated three times, to reject claim 1. The USPTO examiner does not mention the Meade text, he mention only figures. It is impossible to imagine how it is possible to find in the figure exactly word for word the text of my claims. **In**

addition, it is necessary to stress, that my figures were accepted by USPTO.

In the application Pub. No.: US 2003/0071117A1, Meade proposed to control all the appliances of a household with the help of a portable computing device. The USPTO examiner confused and misinterpreted the situation. What I propose is not a change of control devices. I propose to use the cell phone as a main source of input information instead of many existing and different sources. This proposal requires only some relatively simple changes in the phone scheme. However, it gives great convenience and advantages. The goal of complete automation and central control for the entire household in my application is not even mentioned. On the other hand, the goal of elimination of input lines is not mentioned by Meade.

This shows that the examiner, accidentally or intentionally, did not understand the principal differences between my and Meade's applications.

The same should be repeated for claims 2, 4, 7, and 9.

2. For claims 5, 6, 8 and 10, reviewer copied my claims and added "*Meade discloses*", e.g. "*With respect to claim 6: Meade discloses a method according to claim 5 that allows eliminating the necessity of telephone lines and does not bind the telephone position next to the line outlet; the widening of cellular phone usage would make it cheaper* ***(fig.7, parag. 0090-0091)***".

Meade wrote commenting his fig. 7: "*[0016] FIG. 7 is a block diagram of a mobile phone, a land-line phone, and a mobile computing device of an appliance control system, according to one embodiment of the present invention*". In the parag. 0090-0091 Meade did not mention input lines of land-line phone. In these paragraphs, as well as in the rest of his application, there is nothing said about eliminating those lines, the primary goal of my application. Meade treats both types of phones as equivalent devices.

3. For claim 3, "*With respect to claim 3:Meade discloses a method according to claim 1 that allows to receive TV programs and videophone conversations on big TV or PC screens directly through the cellular phone* **(parag. 0027)**, *the cellular phones have such possibilities; today's TV does not; temporarily can be used a coaxial cable output from the cellular phone, or any other available in TV; in the nearest future all digital TV would have a USB input, a USB output from a cellular phone already exists* **(parag. 0027)".**

Page 4

However, Meade's parag. 0027 mentioned a different goal: "*[0027] For example, upon entry within a room, the mobile computing device can automatically perform these steps: identify an appliance like a TV; activate the TV; turn the TV to a channel carrying a favorite program; and select a preferred volume level. In the event that the favorite program is not being broadcast, the mobile computing device can supply its own content. In particular, the mobile computing device can retrieve an episode of that program or substitute a program from memory of the mobile computing device, transfer that stored program to the TV, and then command the appliance to play the program*".

From the above it is obvious that the rejection of claims 1 - 10 based on the Pub. No.: US 2003/0071117A1 is inaccurate. It is completely wrong.

1.2. ANSWER TO THE NEW PARAGRAPH ON PAGE 13

The text, added into the review from 5/17/2010 to the copy of the previous USPTO review from 3/2/2009 is given below. Reviewer placed it as one paragraph of continuous text without intervals on page 13. I beg the reader to inspect the above "criticism" of my point 1, given by the USPTO examiner and determine whether this addition makes any additional sense. However, I cannot ignore the examiner's remark. I divided this text in parts (A1, A2, A3, A4), and after each placed my comment.

A1) *"Applicant's arguments filed 04/0212009 have been fully considered but they are not persuasive. Regarding claim 1, applicant argued that the cited reference did not disclose cell phone or input line, hub, PDA and central control .Applicant also argued that claim 4 was not rejected in the previous rejection and that examiner only copied claim 1 for the rejection of claim 4".*

This is a generality, which confirms the validity of my criticism.

A2) *"Examiner respectfully disagrees with this statement because Meade reference discloses a mobile computing device (fig.2, item 12) operating in an environment of one or more appliances (fig.2, item 13) in which mobile computing device 12 in fig. 2 controls appliance 13, in fig. 2 both mobile computing device 12 and appliance 13 include content 16 and user preferences 18 as in parag.0031".*

Meade application propose: "*A method of controlling an appliance comprises* ***controlling the appliance with at least one of a plurality of mobile computing devices*** *and establishing priority of control over the appliance between the pluralities of mobile computing devices using a priority rule. An appliance control system comprises at least one appliance, a first mobile computing device and a second mobile computing device, each of which includes a priority contention moderator configured for determining and awarding priority over control of the appliance to one of the first and second computing devices".*

Page 5

This is repeated in the Meade claim 1: "*1. A method of controlling an appliance comprising: controlling the appliance* ***with at least one of a plurality of mobile computing devices;*** *and* *establishing priority of control over the appliance between the pluralities of mobile computing devices using a priority rule".*

This is repeated in 0031, which is mentioned by examiner: *"[0031] An appliance control system 10, according to one exemplary embodiment of the present invention, is shown in FIG. 1. Appliance control* ***system 10 includes at least one mobile computing device 12*** *operating in an environment of one or more appliances 13 in which mobile computing device 12 controls appliance 13. Both mobile computing device 12 and appliance 13 include content 16 and user preferences 18. ..."*

The USPTO reviewers either did not understand, or intentionally distorted the sense of both Meade's and my applications:

1. Meade claims the goal of remote control for household appliances through the cell phone and with help of a specialized computer.

2. The goal of my application is conducting an exchange of information with the external world through the cell phone. Now this information is obtained from different sources as telephone lines, cables, and so on.

3. Let us imagine that Meade proposed exactly my solution, but based on completely different technology and by a different method. Does this reject my version? It is known, for example, such a patent. It was proposed to hang up jet engines under airplane wings. All elements of technology existed for a long time.

A3) *"Examiner also rejected claim 4 under 103 (a). Claim 4 depend on claim 1 and the primary reference used for claim 1 does not disclose the limitation of claim 4 so a secondary reference (McZeal) has been used which discloses a cell phone with a webcam (col.21, lines 1-5)".*

1. McZeal pursues other purposes and there is no analogy in the webcam usage.

2. Instead of a cell phone and a webcam as have been used by McZeal, I say that the cell phone may be used instead of a webcam. In 2010 (not in 2005), it is hardly needed.

A4) "*The rejection of claim 1 has been incorporated in claim 4 since it depends on claim 1 and examiner has given the motivation to combine the primary and secondary reference. Every limitation in the claim of the above invention has been rejected based on the references used and the citation has been provided so that the applicant would know where in the references apply to a particular limitation*".

As it is shown above, claim 1 cannot be rejected based on Meade and McZeal claims. This removes (new?) objections against claim 4.

Page 6

PART 2. REMARKS RELATED TO THE FORM OF MY APPLICATION

Remarks on the pages 1 - 7 may be divided into two groups.

The first group is related to the form of the document. For this, a lawyer is not needed. The USPTO rules are clear and could be easily followed. **However, no attorney can make proposals patentable, if they are not a new and an original word in the technology.** If proposed claims are not original, claims must be rejected independently of by whom and with what language they are written. Consequently, according to review, for copying others' proposals, my application is rejected by USPTO. However, USPTO hopes that I will use service of an attorney (their?); what for?

The second group requires clear and precise expression for specific ideas. Here an attorney could be harmful. I tried to get help from attorneys – specialists in patent applications and ran into difficulties such as wordy and vague expressions, which may be easily rejected. However, the most serious problem was the misrepresentation of the idea. When I pointed to such issues, the lawyer agreed. He said that to avoid this, we must work together. This would take much more time and money. On the other hand, I was not given any attorney's remarks about the application's form and language misunderstandings. Analysis of USPTO publications, including all four publications mentioned in my case shows that they must be rejected under the same formal rules and the same reasons. **This allows one to state that USPTO uses these rules very selectively.**

Point 8 (page 12) has an observation about the absence of discussion. In this case, this cannot be applicable. In my answers it is shown that the examiner's observations are contrived and do not refer to the object in consideration. The necessary quotations are given. Actually, the same review was sent several times without the sidelights. This can cause bewilderment, but not a reason for a discussion.

It is necessary to mention that multiple rejections of all the claims due to the necessity of correction the document form is unjust. All the content of pages in USPTO Summaries related to the form of the document is expressed in the following: "*1. An examination of this application reveals that applicant is unfamiliar with patent prosecution procedure. While an inventor may prosecute the application, lack of skill in this field usually acts as a liability in affording the maximum protection for the invention disclosed. Applicant is advised to secure the services of a registered patent attorney or agent to prosecute the application, since the value of a patent is largely dependent upon skilled preparation and prosecution. The Office cannot aid in selecting an attorney or agent.*

A listing of registered patent attorneys ..."

Review from 5/17/10 may be summarized by two phrases:

1. You must be compulsorily turned to an attorney (and, apparently pay solid fee).

2. All the claims in your application 10/905635 from 1/13/05 are rejected. They are not original and are in other previously published applications.

Page 7

In the review, there is a phrase **about the possible need for a payment for the further consideration of the application (page 14). Actually, such a long duration (already more than five years) completely is due to the USPTO.** USPTO needs more than a year for the copying of 15 pages of its previous answer. USPTO requires years for making a copy of a document, which is sent as a new review. The USPTO must compensate the damage. I assume that specialists deal with the review of applications in the USPTO. They must be competent in the object of claims and they must know how to use the USPTO database. For the qualified composition of the answer, it is necessary to carry out the following:

1. Searching the USPTO database by keywords. This requires about an hour. For a lazy idler it would take not more than one day.

2. To copy from the database several points of formal requirements for the patents. Less than one hour is required to do this. For a lazy idler it would take not more than one day.

3. To copy from the previous answer the objections, without worrying about the logic (in my case). Copying without investigating, that these objections are false and do not correspond to reality and completely ignoring the applicant's answer. This requires about an hour. For a lazy idler it would take not more than one day.

Less than a week is sufficient for the composition of a review. However, for the review from May 17, 2010 one day is too much. My previous answer is obtained by USPTO on April

2, 2009. Conclusion to it was sent on May 17, 2010. I.e., it is more than a year. All participating in such "work organization" should be fired for the intentional malicious sabotage.

CONCLUSION

1. In my previous three answers to USPTO, I repeated and demonstrated that none of the reviewer's allegations were found in **Pub. No.: US 2002/0068529A1, Pub. No.: US 2005/0070327A1,** and **Patent No.: US 6763226B1.**

2. It is wrong to reject something because it could be performed ***"by combining with modification"*** of something that already exists. The applications used by reviewers have no description of many devices (some of them are completely new and problematic). However, reviewer states that in my application well-known existing devices are mentioned but not described.

3. Possibly, one additional purpose is pursued. An attorney would write a new application and it would be impossible to prove that it is identical to the one from January 2005. Countdown would begin from the publication of the new application. This one deliberately would be possible to reject by proposals from the applications introduced from 2005 through 2010. It seems that USPTO keeps on file certain applications, which could be used to repel others and then apply with the similar ones.

4. Could the reader believe the facts in my answers? It looks impossible, but it is true. All the three USPTO conclusions, in the smallest degree, do not reject anything in

Page 8

my application. **That is why I could not add anything that defends my application or prove that it deserves a patent.** Refuting anything not connected to the matter under discussion adds nothing. **It is impossible to agree with the USPTO Office Action Summaries from 05/17/2010 to app. No. 10/905635, art unit 2618.**

5. My objections to the criticism of the originality of the positions of my application are not the most important consequence of the present document. I repeated that the reasons, given in the review, were not substantiated. USPTO completely ignored my objections, and repeated the reviews. USPTO does not even mention that my objections are wrong. Only the conclusions were changed: non-final rejection, final rejection, non-final rejection, final rejection (5/17/10). More than five years past and an unknown number of years are in front. The introduction of proposals would lose its utility.

6. Conclusion about the necessity of creating the commission is the most important consequence of the present document. A commission for estimation and averting in the future of the enormous financial and moral damage, done to the United States of America, by the USPTO actions. For example, it is difficult to find a task or process, which cannot be carried out by a modern computer. In the USPTO opinion, since in Meade claim there is a phrase ***"controlling the appliance with at least one of a plurality of mobile computing devices"*** all further improvements of the computer technology application and means of automation must come to the USA after being patented in other countries.

An application related to rapidly developing technology loses its usefulness with time. My application was given in January 2005. I obtained, on 10/22/2007 non-final rejection; on 8/29/2008 final rejection; on 3/2/2009 non-final rejection, on 5/17/2010 final rejection. In the subsequent answers entire pages from the first answer were copied, i.e., were repeated.

USPTO text deliberately does not correspond to the reality of the application proposals.

In the copy from 05/17/10, it is not copied only the first phrase from the previous review from 03/02/2009, *"Application request for reconsideration of the finality of the rejection of the last Office action is persuasive and, therefore, the finality of this action is withdrawn"*. **It is interesting to understand how and why the USPTO changes its opinion. USPTO Action Summaries and my answers repeated the same text.** I focus the attention to the fact that I am angry about the USPTO work, but I never requested about the removal of the final rejection to a non-final one. It can seem when reading this document that the author uses sharp expressions. Please, do consider that more than for five years many times I was required to reply to the same text copied from the previous USPTO Action Summaries. My responses, which show that the USPTO assertions are false, are completely ignored.

Enormous financial and moral damage, which follows from the USPTO actions, must be ended. **With this purpose, it is necessary to create a commission on the level of Congress and Attorney General, which would find out:**

Page 9

1. The state and organization of the work of the USPTO.

2. The damage, which is brought by USPTO actions, to the economy and to the image of the USA. Simultaneously it would be good to compare how much this damage exceeds the damage from, for example, terrorism, including expenditures for preventing terrorist acts.

3. Whether this objectively existing damage is the result of intentional actions.

4. How the categorical demand of enormous payment to the lawyers is compulsory. To what extent this requirement is unselfish.

Sincerely Ilya Kogan

3.12. USPTO letter from 11-29-2010.

UNITED STATES PATENT AND TRADEMARK OFFICE

COMMISSIONER FOR PATENTS

NOV 29 2010

Mr. Ilya Kogan
2573 E 27 St.
Brooklyn, NY 11235

Dear Mr. Kogan:

Thank you for your communication of August 20, 2010, addressed to the Secretary of Commerce, the Honorable Gary Locke, and the communication of June 20, 2010 addressed to the Inspector General of the U.S. Department of Commerce regarding your patent application (10/905,635). Your communication has been refined to me in the Office of the Commissioner for Patents to prepare a response.

Your communications express your dissatisfaction with the treatment that you have received by the United States Patent and Trademark Office (USPTO) with regards to Patent Application
10/905,635 and the time it takes for the USPTO to respond.

In addressing your concern for timeliness, while there was a delay in addressing your response filed November 16, 2007, which we apologize for, all other communications up to May 17, 2010, appear timely. In reviewing your application, we see that a final rejection was mailed on May 17, 2010 and a reply from you was received on June 7, 2010. Since the Office did not act on your reply until after November 17, 2010, your application is now abandoned. We apologize for this delay.

In discussions with the Office of Petitions, if you wish to continue prosecution of application serial number 10/905,635, it must be returned to pending status. It may be possible to revive the application by filing a petition pursuant to Title 37 of the Code of Federal Regulations (CFR) §1.137. Specifically, there are two options available under 37 CPR §1.117 that may enable an applicant to have an abandoned application revived.

37 CFR § 1. 137(a) sets forth if the delay in reply by applicant was unavoidable, a petition may be filed pursuant to this paragraph to revive an abandoned application. A grantable petition pursuant to this paragraph must be accompanied by: (1) The reply required to the outstanding Office Action or notice, unless previously filed; (2) The petition fee as set forth in § 1.17(1) (currently $270.00 for small entity; $540.00 for non-small entity); and (3) A showing to the satisfaction of the Director that the entire delay in filing the required reply from the due date for the reply until the filing of a grantable petition pursuant to this paragraph was unavoidable.

The second option for revival is available under 37 CFR § 1.137(b) which sets forth that if the delay in reply by applicant was unintentional, a petition may be filed pursuant to this paragraph to revive an abandoned application. A grantable petition pursuant to this paragraph must be accompanied by: (1) The reply required to the outstanding Office Action or notice, unless previously filed; (2) The petition fee as set forth in § 1.17(m) (currently $810.00 for small entity: $1,620.00 for non-small entity); and (3) A statement that the entire delay in filing the required reply from the due date for the reply until the filing of a grantable petition pursuant to this paragraph was unintentional. The Director may require additional information where there is a question whether the delay was unintentional.

Should you decide to proceed with the filing of a petition under 37 CFR § 1.137(a) or (b), the petition should be mailed to:

Mail Stop Petition
Commissioner for Patents
P.O. Box 1450
Alexandria, VA 22313-1450
Or by FAX:
571-273-8300
Attn: Office of Petitions

If you do successfully revive your application, it is noted that the Office actions you have received in your application clearly set forth that your claims do not meet the requirements for patentability. For example, many of your claims are not in the proper format, which requires a single sentence. It is noted that you have not mended any of your claims throughout the prosecution. It appears that you and the examiner are at an impasse regarding the patentability of claims in the application. The Office has a procedure for such and the of patent Appeals and Interferences (BPAI). In an appeal, a panel of three administrative patent judges from the BPAI reviews the claim rejections and decides whether the applicant or the examiner is correct.

An appeal is apriority ate when the applicant and the examiner are at odds regarding the patentability of the claims in an application. An appeal can be filed at any time after an examiner rejects at least one claim twice. In your situation, you appear to believe that your claims are sufficiently distinguished from the prior art and need no further amendment, yet the examiner has persisted in rejecting your claims. Since a final rejection was mailed on May 17, 2010, the claims in your application have been rejected at least twice. You therefore have the option of appealing the examiner's rejection of your claims. If you truly believe your claims to be patentable, you should follow the correct procedure and file an appeal.

For information regarding the filing of an appeal to the BPAI, please refer to chapter 1200 of the manual of Patent Examining Procedure (MPEP). The MPEP can be found at the following Web address:
http://www.uspto.gov/web/offices/pac/mpep/index.htm

In addition, it is noted that you are prosecuting the application yourself. Although a registered attorney or agent is not required, the USPTO strongly encourages the use of a registered patent attorney or agent for assistance in drafting, filing, or prosecuting patent applications. The patent application process is complex, and many inventors find the assistance of a registered attorney or agent very helpful. Although the USPTO cannot recommend any particular attorney or agent we do maintain a roster of patent attorneys and agents registered to practice before the USPTO. Only registered attol1leys and agents may help others to obtain patents. A roster of registered attorneys and agents can be found at
http://des.uspto.gov/OEDCI/GeoRegion.jsp.

In addition, it is appreciated that you may desire to forgo the services of a registered attorney or agent. As a result, another available avenue for assistance would be to contact our Inventors Assistance Center (lAC), information of which may be found on our Web site at: (http://www.uspto.gov/).

The lAC provides patent information and services to the public. The Office is staffed by former Supervisory Patent Examiners and experienced Primary Examiners who answer general questions concerning patent examining policy and procedure.

HOW TO CONTACT THE lAC

Telephone Numbers
800-PTO-9199, (800-786-9199), 571-272-1000
TTY - customers can dial 571-272-9950
for customer assistance.

Hours of Operation
Monday - Friday; 8:30 AM - 5:30 PM (ET)

The lAC will not be staffed during Government holidays. When the USPTO closes early (for example, due to weather conditions) the lAC will also cease operations.

I hope this letter addresses your request. If you have any further questions relating to this matter, please contact Larry R. Helms at (571) 272-8800.

Sincerely,
(signature)
Anthony Caputa
Office of the Commissioner for patents

3.13. My response to the USPTO letter from 11-29-2010

To: Secretary of US DoC Gary Locke
U.S. Department of Commerce
1401 Constitution Ave., NW Washington, DC 20230
Copy TheSec@doc.gov

USPTO usptoinfo@uspto.gov

From: Ilya Kogan
kogani@optonline.net 718/769-8637
2573 E 27 St., Brooklyn NY 11235

Re: Letter from USPTO dated November 29, 2010 (no registration number), signed by Anthony Caputa.

Firstly, I want to stress that this letter is not relevant to the patentability of my application number 10/905, 635. Nevertheless, it should be noted that more than five years, USPTO has not a single reason, which denies the originality of the application claims. That should be enough for approval.

The USPTO letter contains three pages in which are described the procedure under which I can apply for reconsideration. However, I must first pay $ 1.137. The procedure is described in detail. The essence of the letter extensively described in the first few lines.

"Thank you for your communication on August 20, 2010, addressed to the Secretary of Commerce the Honorable Gary Locke, and the communication of June 20, 2010 addressed to the Inspector General of the U.S. Department of Commerce regarding your patent application (10/905,635). …
(7 lines of general text with ", which we apologize for,")

... In reviewing your application, we see that the final rejection was mailed on May 17, 2010 and a reply from you was received from you on June 7, 2010. **Since office did not act on your reply until after November 17, 2010, your application is now abandoned. We apologize for this delay."**

Full text of the USPTO letter, this answer, and all other materials posted on http://speculations.us/InIndex/Notebook/History_and_Remarks.htm

Such a response may be understood as a mockery. Including a mockery of the high addressees referred to, due to which the answer is written. From the answer, I do not understand why I should pay $ 1.137. **Logical is to expect from the USPTO a much greater amount and additional apologies.** This is a complete answer to the letter. Add my outrage think superfluous. However, confident that everyone would agree with me, who would acquainted with the materials on the above website.

Mr. Locke, the site of your department (http://www.commerce.gov/about-department-commerce) proclaims, "The U.S. Department of Commerce has a broad mandate to advance economic growth and jobs and opportunities for the American people". The USPTO, your subordinate, obviously acts in the opposite direction. My case is a small, however, a proving example.

Sincerely Ilya Kogan
December 2, 2010

Appendix, my answer from June 2 to the USPTO document from May 17. See: http://speculations.us/InIndex/Notebook/Answ100517.htm

3.14. 12-02-2010 USPTO Document

The USPTO letter has three pages (two tables and a page with text)

Page 1 ---------------------------------------

UNITED STATES PATENT AND TRADEMARK OFFICE

UNITED STATES DEPARTMENT OF COMMERCE
Address: United States Patent
And Trademark Office
COMMISSIONER FOR PATENTS
P.O. Bo.' 1450
Alexandria. Virginia 22313-1450
www.uspto.gov

Application No 101905,635
FILLING DATE *01/13/2005*

FIRST NAMED INVENTOR Ilya Kogan
CONFIRMATION NO. 2635
50602 7590

ILYA KOGAN
2573 E. 27TH ST.
BROOKLYN, NY 11235

EXAMINER AKINYEMI, AJIBOLA A
ART UNIT 2618 Mail Date *12/09/2010*

Please find below and/or attached an Office communication concerning this application or proceeding.

The time period for reply, if any, is set in the attached communication.

Page 2 ------------------------------------
(Copied only marked with **[X]** positions)

Advisory Action
Before the Filing **of** *an Appeal Brief*

Application No. 10/905,635
Examiner AJIBOLA AKINYEMI
Applicant(s) KOGAN, ILYA
Art Unit 2618

-- *The MAILING DATE of this communication appears on the cover sheet with the correspondence address*--

THE REPLY FILED 07 June 2010 FAILS TO PLACE THIS APPLICATION IN CONDITION FOR ALLOWANCE.

1. **[X]** The reply was filed after a final rejection, but prior to or on the same day as filing a Notice of Appeal. To avoid abandonment of this application, applicant must timely file one of the following replies: (1) an amendment, affidavit, or other evidence, which places the application in condition for allowance; (2) a Notice of Appeal (with appeal fee) in compliance with 37 CFR 41.31; or (3) a Request for Continued Examination (RCE) in compliance with 37 CFR 1.114. The reply must be filed within one of the following time periods:

b) **[X]**The period for reply expires on: (1) the mailing date of this Advisory Action, or (2) the date set forth in the final rejection, whichever is later. In no event, however, will the statutory period for reply expire later than SIX MONTHS from the mailing date of the final rejection.

Examiner Note: If box 1 is checked, check either box (a) or (b). ONLY CHECK BOX (b) WHEN THE FIRST REPLY WAS FILED WITHIN TWO MONTHS OF THE FINAL REJECTION. See MPEP 706.07(f).

Extensions of time may be obtained under 37 CFR 1.136(a). The date on which the petition under 37 CFR 1.136(a) and the appropriate extension fee have been filed is the date for purposes of determining the period of extension and the corresponding amount of the fee. The appropriate extension fee under 37 CFR 1.17(a) is calculated from: (1) the expiration date of the shortened statutory period for reply originally set in the final Office action; or (2) as set forth in (b) above, if checked. Any reply received by the Office later than three months after the mailing date of the final rejection, even if timely filed, may reduce any earned patent term adjustment. See 37 CFR 1. 704(b).

7. **[X]** For purposes of appeal, the proposed amendment(s): b) **[X]** will be entered and an explanation of how the new or amended claims would be rejected is provided below or appended.

The status of the claim(s) is (or will be) as follows:
Claim(s) allowed:__.
Claim(s) objected to: __.
Claim(s) rejected: ***1-10.***
Claim(s) withdrawn from consideration:__.

REQUEST FOR RECONSIDERATION/OTHER

11. **[X]** The request for reconsideration has been considered but does NOT place the application in condition for allowance because:

See Continuation Sheet.

12. **[X]** Note the attached Information *Disclosure Statement(s)*. (PTO/S8/0B) Paper NO(s).__

/Duc Nguyen/
Supervisory Patent Examiner, Art Unit 2618

Page 3 -----------------------------------

Continuation Sheet (PTO-303)
Application No. *10/905,635*

Continuation of 11. does NOT place the application in condition for allowance because: Applicant argued that (1)... Meade and his application have completely different goals and from the point of view of their priority and the concept of the invention do not interfere with each other. Applicant also argued (2). that all of his claim are copied and that examiner only put the word "Meade discloses" in front of it as if he copies his claim from somewhere else. (3) He argued that examiner does not mention Meade Text but only figures, which makes it impossible to understand Meade application or invention. (4) He argued that the examiner did not understand or confused and misinterpreted his invention, which is the use of cell phone as a main source of input information instead of many existing and different source.

(5) ...Applicant argued that Meade and McZeal do not disclose the use of cell phone as a webcam. Examiner respectfully disagrees with all this statements:

(1) Meade reference and the instant invention are similar and Meade anticipates the claim languages of the present invention, which is using a wireless device such as PDA, cellular phone as a HUB. Applicant argues that Meade does not mention about the words: phone, telephone, hub or PDA. However, para 26 of Meade clearly states that the mobile computing device 12 can be a personal digital assistant (PDA).

(2) Examiner did not mention that applicant copied the claim from any source but examiner is only trying to explain how the claim has been anticipated by Meade reference using the word "Meade discloses" in front of the claim language.

(3) Examiner also uses figures, which is the best way of pointing out the physical aspect of Meade's invention to the applicant. Examiner believes that using figures and little explanation is the best way of explaining the cited reference and the way it anticipates the claimed invention.

(4) Examiner cited fig.2, item 12 in the office action. Item 12 is a wireless PDA in which Meade reference used to control all the appliances 13 as in parag.0011, 0034 and 0039. This PDA serves as a hub for all the appliances as in the cited paragraph.

(5) Meade in combination with McZeal discloses the use of cell phone as a webcam as disclose in the last office action, McZeal discloses a phone with webcam in (co1.21, lines 1-5). This reference is being combined with the primary reference, which is Meade that discloses the remaining limitation of claim 4 as cited in the last office action.

Applicant fails to respond to the rejections made under 35 USC 112 and 101. For instance, the claims are written in a narrative form that does not clearly spell out exactly what the claims are intended to recite. In addition, there are grammatical errors in the claims that create confusion as to what is exactly being claimed. These errors need to be corrected so that the claims will be more clearly understood. In addition, the claims are directed to a process ("method"), but no definitive steps are recited that describe how the process is to be implemented. The claims should be rewritten to recite definitive steps; MPEP 2173. 05(q)

Another problem with the claims is that many of them are not in a one-sentence format. Most of them contain more than one sentence. It is required that each claim begins with a capital letter and end with a period. Periods may not be used elsewhere in the claims except for abbreviations. MPEP 608.01 (m)

3.15. My response to the USPTO document from 12/02/2010

Page 1 of 3

To: Commissioner for Patents,
US Patent and Trademark Office
P.O. Box 1450, Alexandria, VA 22313 - 1450

From: Ilya Kogan
2573 E 27 St., Brooklyn NY 11235,
kogani@optonline.net, 718-769-8637

Re: USPTO document from December 2, 2010
About application # 10/905,635

December 5, 2010

1. An analysis of formal requirements

1.1. From the filing of the application (050113) to the last answer (101202) elapsed more than 70 months. During this time, the USPTO has sent me the first response (with an original text), three copies of it in the following responses, and the document that is answering. It took USPTO about 67 months (70 - 3).Thus, after six years of which I have used three months, and the rest USPTO, I am declared that I have to ask for an extension of the application and pay for it. Permissible in a letter vocabulary would not allow expressing outrage.

1.2. USPTO has formal requirements. For example, it is stated that some of the sentences in the application should be replaced by one. This is done by replacing the points with a semicolon, which certainly must be done.

However, all items of the application are rejected because they are not original and are introduced in other applications. That is, USPTO routinely insists that these formal changes can make not original claims patentable. This is an absurd.

2. Responding to the examiner's main remarks

2.1. USPTO intentionally or through ignorance does not see the differences:
- To use Cell phone or computer to control the switching of various devices, and
- To use Cell phone as a source of information that currently many devices obtain from other sources such as antenna or cable.

Meade application offers to manage the switching of these devices and says nothing about changing information sources. My application is to replace the sources of Information and does not address device switching. You can switch on any device, e.g. TV, but if it has not a cable with information, the screen would be empty.

2.2. The document under consideration is not an exact copy of previous USPTO responses. In it, approximately one-third of a page is not copied it is rewritten from

Page 2 of 3

previous responses USPTO. I have responded to this several times. However, examiner may pretend that this is something new and I do answer.

Examiner wrote (all the examiner's text is as it is written by examiner), "*(1) Meade reference and the instant invention are similar and Meade anticipates the claim languages of the present invention which is using a wireless device such as PDA, cellular phone and a Hub. Applicant argues that Meade does not mention about the words: phone, telephone, hub or PDA. However, para 26 Meade clearly states that the mobile computing device 12 can be personal digital assistant (PDA)."*

Copy of Meade paragraph 26, *"[0026] An appliance control system of the present invention enables a mobile computing device, such as a personal digital assistant, to control appliances like televisions, radios, printers, etc. The control can take several forms including applying preferences to the appliance such as volume level, activation and deactivation along with determining the content available to the appliance such as supplying a program, song, or file to be acted upon by the appliance. In addition, control can include simply selecting available content to be used by the appliance, such as selecting a TV channel or regularly broadcast program."*

The above Meade text confirms, that my and Meade applications are misinterpreted by USPTO. Meade's goal is to switch, not to work with information. Meade does not mention in the text or in the pictures the information sources.

Examiner wrote, *"(2) Examiner did not mention that applicant copied the claim from any source but examiner is only trying to explain how the claim has been anticipated by Meade reference using the words "Meade discloses" in front of the claim language".*

Such style is not allowed. It is used for making for sure false conclusions. To add before copy of my claim two words "Meade discloses", proves nothing. It must be some explanation why it is so.

Examiner wrote, *"(3) Examiner also uses figures which is the best way of pointing out the physical aspect of Meade's invention to the applicant. Examiner believes that using figures and little explanation is the best way of explaining the cited reference and the way it anticipates the claimed invention.*

(4) Examiner cited fig.2, item 12 in the office action. Item 12 is a wireless PDA in which Meade reference used to control all the appliances 13 as in parag.0011, 0034 and 0039. This PDA serves as a hub for all the appliances as in the cited paragraph."

There is no "a little explanation" as examiner writes. The interpretation of drawings by the examiner does not correspond to their description in the Meade application. The examiner does (intentionally?) false conclusions without confirming them with text.

Page 3 of 3

Examiner wrote, "*(5) Meade in combining with McZeal discloses the use of cell phone as a webcam as disclose in the last office action, McZeal discloses a phone with webcam in (col.21, lines 1-5). This reference is being combined with the primary reference which is Meade that discloses the remaining limitation of claim 4 as cited in the last office action".*

USPTO insists (repeatedly) that if you combine different sources (e.g., Meade application and McZeal patent), then we can get some of my application. This is not true when applied to the particular case. However, this is wrong in principal. Combining of different patents can be patentable. Both McZeal patent and Meade application combine devices, which are known (and patented) for a long time. E.g., Meade proposes to control switches, known by years with computers and phones known by years; to say nothing that the computers and phones are in use for such purpose for a long time.

3. Conclusion

3.1. USPTO document contains no new material. It attempts in a few phrases repeated many times in the past to

confirm their point of view. However, the document in any way cannot serve as an additional justification for knowingly false and repeated several times in copies the first USPTO answer.

There is an issue of compensation for moral and financial damages caused to me personally (this is not associated with patentability of my application); however this is not related to the matters dealt with herein.

3.2. In paragraph 1.1 is shown that the USPTO work does irreparable harm to the United States of America. Such tremendous delays lead to great financial damages caused by delay in the introduction of new technologies; it is contributing to the technological backwardness of the United States. This is a huge moral damage to the country.

This response, the document from the USPTO on Dec. 2, 2010, and other materials relating to this issue are on the site

http://speculations.us/InIndex/Notebook/History_and_Remarks.htm

These documents can be found on the website USPTO.

Sincerely Ilya Kogan

3.16. USPTO letter from 12/09/2010

The USPTO letter has two pages (two tables)

Page 1 --

UNITED STATES PATENT AND TRADEMARK OFFICE

UNITED STATES DEPARTMENT OF COMMERCE
Address: United States Patent
and Trademark Office
COMMISSIONER
FOR PATENTS
P.O. Bo.' 1450
Alexandria. Virginia 22313-1450

www.uspto.gov

Application No 101905,635   FILING DATE *01/13/2005*

FIRST NAMED NVENTOR Ilya Kogan
CONFIRMATION NO. 2635
50602 7590

ILYA KOGAN
2573 E. 27TH ST.
BROOKLYN, NY 11235

EXAMINER AKINYEMI, AJIBOLA A
ART UNIT 2618 Mail Date *12/09/2010*

Please find below and/or attached an Office communication concerning this application or proceeding.

The time period for reply, if any, is set in the attached communication.

Page 2 ------------------------------------
(Copied only marked with **[X]** positions)
Notice of *Abandonment*
Application No. 10/905,635
Examiner AJIBOLA AKINYEMI
Applicant(s) KOGAN, ILYA
Art Unit 2618
-- *The MAILING DATE of this communication appears on the cover sheet with the correspondence address--*

This application is abandoned in view of:
1. **[X]** Applicant's failure to timely file a proper reply to the Office letter mailed on 17 *May 2010.*
(b) **[X]** A proposed reply was received on *07 June 2010,* but it does not constitute a proper reply under 37 CFR 1.113 (a) to the final rejection.
(A proper reply under 37 CFR 1.113 to a final rejection consists only of: (1) a timely filed amendment, which places, the
application in condition for allowance; (2) a timely filed Notice of Appeal (with appeal fee); or (3) a timely filed Request for
Continued Examination (RCE) in compliance with 37 CFR 1.114).
.....
7. **[X]** The reason(s) below:
The period for properly responding to the final office action mailed 05/17/2010 was expired on 11/17/2010
/Duc Nguyen/
Supervisory Patent Examiner, Art Unit 2618
Petitions to revive under 37 CFR 1.137(a) or (b), or requests to withdraw the holding of abandonment under 37 CFR

1.181, should be promptly filed to minimize any negative effects on patent term.

U.S. Patent and Trademark Office

PTOL-1432 (Rev. 04-01) Notice of Abandonment Part of Paper No. 20101208

3.17. My response to the USPTO letter from 12/09/2010

--

December 17, 2010

To: Attorney General of the United States
Eric H. Holder Jr.
U.S. Department of Justice
950 Pennsylvania Avenue, NW
Washington, DC 20530-0001

Copy: Secretary of US DoC Gary Locke
TheSec@doc.gov
USPTO usptoinfo@uspto.gov

From: Ilya Kogan
2573 E 27 St., Brooklyn NY 11235,
kogani@optonline.net, 718-769-8637

Re: USPTO document from December 9, 2010
About application # 10/905,635

Dear Mister Holder,

In January 2005, I filed an application to the USPTO. For the six years, it was identified at least, very strange USPTO actions.

All items of my application are rejected, as repetitions of items of other applications. This is false. In my responses, I give solid arguments that the USPTO statements have nothing to do with my application. From the USPTO in response I get copies of their first response, without any additional comments, **an exact copy not a similar text.**

After six years, of which I have used three months for my answers, and the rest USPTO, I have not received any critical comments on the merits of my proposal. Thus, six years cannot say what deserves my application. There is reason to believe that my case is not unique. Apparently, there is a type of applications in respect of which the USPTO operates the same way.

USPTO actions cause great economic and moral damage to the U.S. I appeal to you, hoping to stop such actions. I see no other methods to stop such arbitrariness, but prosecutors and the media. I have repeatedly offered to create a commission that would investigate USPTO work, to determine the motives, effects and damage from such actions.

The documents can be found on the website USPTO. This letter, the document from the USPTO on Dec. 9, 2010, and other materials relating to this issue are on the site **http://speculations.us/InIndex/Notebook/History_and_Remarks.htm**

Sincerely Ilya Kogan

3.18. USPTO letter from 12/20/2010

UNITED STATES PATENT AND TRADEMARK OFFICE

COMMISSIONER FOR PATENTS

DEC 20 2010

Mr. Ilya Kogan
2573 E 27 Street
Brooklyn, NY 11235

Dear Mr. Kogan:

Thank you for your e-mail of December 2, 2010, addressed to the Secretary of Commerce, the Honorable Gary Locke, and your e-mail of December 17, 2010, addressed to the Attorney General of the United States, the Honorable Mr. Eric H. Holder, Jr., regarding your patent application (10/905,635). Your correspondence has been referred to me in the Office of the Commissioner for Patents.

Your communication expresses your dissatisfaction with the treatment you received from the United States Patent and Trademark Office (USPTO) with regards to Patent Application Number 10/905,635. It appears that you feel the letter mailed to you on November 29, 2010 was not relevant to the patentability of your application. Further, you question why you must pay additional fees.

It may prove helpful to review the facts of the case. A final Office action was mailed to you on May 17, 2010. A final

Office action is given when the examiner has made a final determination as to the patentability of the claims of the application. The rules of the USPTO limit the actions that you may take following a final Office action. An applicant faced with a final Office action may take anyone of the following options: 1) file a notice of appeal and appeal brief; 2) file a request for continued examination, commonly called an RCE; 3) file a continuation application; 4) request

... *(Two lines lost)*

I hope this letter addresses your request. If you have any further questions relating to this matter, please contact Larry R. Helms at (571) 272-8800.

Sincerely,

(signature)

Anthony Caputa
Office of the Commissioner for Patents

3.19. My response to the USPTO letter from 12/20/2010

December 23, 2010

To: Under Secretary of Commerce
for Intellectual Property and Director
of the USPTO **David Kappos**
usptoinfo@uspto.gov

From: Ilya Kogan
2573 E 27 St., Brooklyn NY 11235,
kogani@optonline.net, 718-769-8637

Re: USPTO document from December 20, 2010 signed by **Anthony Caputa** (application # 10/905,635)

Dear Mister Kappos,

In January 2005, I filed an application to the USPTO. For the six years, it was identified at least, very strange USPTO actions.

The documents are on the USPTO website and on the site **http://speculations.us/InIndex/Notebook/History_and_Remarks.htm**

Letter of 12/20/10 written as if USPTO, in this case, performed their duties properly. In fact, USPTO actions over the past six years could be described as actions of an omni powerful bureaucrat whom all is permitted. For this reason, I look forward to the following:

1. A qualified analysis of the USPTO work related to the application # 10/905, 635 must be done.

2. All USPTO actions for the past six years as unrelated to the application # 10/905, 635, and in addition as rough, inconsistent and unskilled; must be canceled

3. Measures adequate to the case must be taken.

Sincerely Ilya Kogan

3.20. USPTO letter from 01/06/2011

UNITED STATES PATENT AND TRADEMARK OFFICE

COMMISSIONER FOR PATENTS

JAN - 6 2011

Mr. Ilya Kogan
2573 E 27 Street
Brooklyn, NY 11235

Dear Mr. Kogan:

Thank you for your communication of December 23, 2010, addressed to the Under Secretary of Commerce for Intellectual Property and Director of the United States Patent and Trademark Office (USPTO), Mr. David Kappos, regarding your patent application (10/905,635). Your communication has been referred to me. In the Office of the Commissioner for Patents for response.

In your communication, you request the Office analyze your application for the work performed by the USPTO and all USPTO actions that are rough, inconsistent, and unskilled be canceled.

Your application's status is now abandoned. As pointed out in the letter mailed to you on December 20, 2010, " ... until such time as the application is revived, no further consideration of the claims will be made by the examiner." In order for us to examine your application and determine whether the invention described in your application meets the statutory requirements for patentability, *you must file a petition under* 37 *CFR* 1. *137(a) or (b) to revive* your application.

You should also note that the Office provides resources to assist independent inventors like you. Please feel free to contact our Inventors Assistance Center (IAC) using the contact information presented below or the independent inventor resources available to you' on our Web site at http://www.uspto.gov/web/offices/pac/dapp/pacmain.html.

The IAC provides patent information and services to the public. The experienced staff of the IAC consists of former Supervisory Patent Examiners and retired Primary Patent Examiners who answer general questions concerning patent examining policy and procedure.

HOW TO CONTACT THE IAC

Telephone Numbers	**Hours of Operation**
800-PTO-9199	Monday - Friday
(800-786-9199)	8:30 AM - 5:30 PM (ET)
571-272-1000;	The JAC will not be staffed during Government holidays. When the USPTO closes early (for example. due to weather conditions) the IAC will also cease operations.

I hope this letter addresses your request. If you have any further questions relating to this matter, please contact Larry R. Helms at (571) 272-8800.

Sincerely,
(signature)
Anthony Caputa

3.21. My response to the USPTO letter from 01/06/2011

January 10, 2011

To: Under Secretary of Commerce
for Intellectual Property and Director
of the USPTO **David Kappos**
usptoinfo@uspto.gov

From: Ilya Kogan
2573 E 27 St., Brooklyn NY 11235,
kogani@optonline.net, 718-769-8637

Re: USPTO document from January 6, 2011
signed by **Anthony Caputa**
(application # 10/905,635)

Dear Mister Kappos,

Second time I apply to you with the same question. In January 2005, I filed an application to the USPTO. For the six years, it was identified at least, very strange USPTO actions. **The very first thing, it is necessary to detach all the persons who are related to the matter with my application. For last six years, they behaved as unqualified bureaucrats. Currently they continue to defend their unqualified and improper decisions.**

The documents are on the USPTO website and on the site **http://speculations.us/InIndex/Notebook/History_and_Remarks.htm**

The letter of 01/06/11 as the letter of 12/20/10 written as if USPTO, in this case, performed their duties properly. In fact, USPTO actions over the past six years could be described as actions of an omni powerful bureaucrat whom all is permitted. For this reason, I look forward to the following:

1. A qualified analysis of the USPTO work related to the application #10/905, 635 must be done. I am sure, that USPTO has qualified specialists.

2. All USPTO actions for the past six years as unrelated to the application #10/905, 635, and in addition as rough, inconsistent and unskilled; must be canceled

3. Measures adequate to the case must be taken.

Sincerely Ilya Kogan

3.22. Letter to Attorney General and WSJ sent 02/26/2011

February 26, 2011

To: Attorney General of the United States
Eric H. Holder Jr.
U.S. Department of Justice
950 Pennsylvania Avenue, NW
Washington, DC 20530-0001
(Not the first time)

To: The Wall Street Journal
onlinejournal@wsj.com

Copy: Secretary of US DoC Gary Locke
U.S. Department of Commerce
1401 Constitution Ave., NW Washington, DC 20230
TheSec@doc.gov

Copy: Under Secretary of Commerce
for Intellectual Property and Director
of the USPTO David Kappos
usptoinfo@uspto.gov

From: Ilya Kogan
2573 E 27 St., Brooklyn NY 11235,
kogani@optonline.net, 718-769-8637

Re: USPTO work on application # 10/905,635, filled 01/13/2005

After more than six years, of which I have used three months for my answers, and the rest (about six years) USPTO, I have not received any critical comments on the merits of my proposal. All items of my application are rejected, as repetitions of items of other applications. This is false. In my responses, I give arguments that the USPTO statements have nothing to do with reality. From the USPTO in response I get copies of their first response, without any additional comments. Thus, I cannot say what deserves my application. There is reason to believe that my case is not unique. USPTO actions cause great economic and moral damage to the U.S. I appeal to you, hoping to stop such actions.

It is not attached the case description that would require dozens of pages. However, no sensible person would believe it, regardless of the conception on the officials' corruption and permissiveness. It would be required to turn to the original documents. In this regard, in addition to the USPTO site, is created a website, where one can find the necessary documents **http://speculations.us/InIndex/Notebook/History_and_Remarks.htm**

I apply to the mass media for the following:

1. To attract attention to the case.

2. To help with organization of a judicial trial. I am an aged pensioner and have no resources to do it myself.

I am looking forward to the following from the General Attorney:

1. All USPTO actions for the past six years as unrelated to the application #10/905,635, and in addition as rough, inconsistent and unskilled; must be canceled

2. A qualified analysis of the USPTO work related to the application #10/905,635 must be done. I am sure, that USPTO has qualified specialists.

Sincerely Ilya Kogan

www.ingramcontent.com/pod-product-compliance
Lightning Source LLC
Chambersburg PA
CBHW051905170526
45168CB00001B/254

* 9 7 8 1 5 1 4 7 1 3 4 2 6 *